Theoretical Cybersecurity

Principles and Advanced Concepts

Dr. Jacob G. Oakley
Michael Butler
Wayne York
Dr. Matthew Puckett
Dr. J. Louis Sewell

Apress®

Theoretical Cybersecurity: Principles and Advanced Concepts

Dr. Jacob G. Oakley
Owens Cross Roads, AL, USA

Dr. Matthew Puckett
Huntsville, AL, USA

Michael Butler
Arlington, VA, USA

Dr. J. Louis Sewell
Huntsville, AL, USA

Wayne York
Owens Cross Roads, AL, USA

ISBN-13 (pbk): 978-1-4842-8299-1   ISBN-13 (electronic): 978-1-4842-8300-4
https://doi.org/10.1007/978-1-4842-8300-4

Managing Director, Apress Media LLC: Welmoed Spahr
Acquisitions Editor: Susan McDermott
Development Editor: Laura Berendson
Coordinating Editor: Jessica Vakili

Distributed to the book trade worldwide by Springer Science+Business Media New York, 233 Spring Street, 6th Floor, New York, NY 10013. Phone 1-800-SPRINGER, fax (201) 348-4505, e-mail orders-ny@springer-sbm.com, or visit www.springeronline.com. Apress Media, LLC is a California LLC and the sole member (owner) is Springer Science + Business Media Finance Inc (SSBM Finance Inc). SSBM Finance Inc is a **Delaware** corporation.

For information on translations, please e-mail booktranslations@springernature.com; for reprint, paperback, or audio rights, please e-mail bookpermissions@springernature.com.

Apress titles may be purchased in bulk for academic, corporate, or promotional use. eBook versions and licenses are also available for most titles. For more information, reference our Print and eBook Bulk Sales web page at http://www.apress.com/bulk-sales.

Any source code or other supplementary material referenced by the author in this book is available to readers on the Github repository: https://github.com/Apress/Theoretical-Cybersecurity. For more detailed information, please visit http://www.apress.com/source-code.

Printed on acid-free paper

Table of Contents

About the Authors

Dr. Jacob G. Oakley is a cybersecurity author and subject matter expert with 16 years of experience focusing on strategic enterprise-level cybersecurity architectures as well as offensive cybersecurity operations within government and commercial sectors. His previous technical books, *Professional Red Teaming*, *Waging Cyber War*, and *Cybersecurity for Space*, are also published by Apress.

Michael Butler is a cybersecurity subject matter expert with 12 years of experience focusing on building, developing, and leading teams of ethical hackers. He is a primary instructor and developer of an offensive cloud security course taught both privately and at Blackhat conferences in the United States, Europe, and Asia. He has previously collaborated with Dr. Oakley as the technical reviewer for *Professional Red Teaming*.

Wayne York is a cybersecurity technical editor and subject matter expert with 18 years of experience focusing on offensive cybersecurity operations and program protection within government and commercial sectors. His previous technical edited book is *Waging Cyber War* by Dr. Oakley, published by Apress.

Dr. Matthew Puckett is a mathematics professor and former software engineer. His areas of interest include theology, cognitive science, and artificial intelligence. His hobbies include chess, where he is currently one of the top 300 players in the United States (according to FIDE).

Dr. J. Louis Sewell is a mathematician trained in Graph Theory. As Technical Fellow of a Huntsville, AL, technology company, he develops enduring solutions to critical infrastructure challenges in government and civilian sectors. Professionally and personally, he has a special interest in artificial intelligence ethics, infinite game dynamics, and the role of personal experience in the philosophy of science.

About the Technical Reviewer

Nathan Kehn is a US Navy service member with over 12 years of operational experience. He has spent his time supporting US Navy Special Warfare and Department of Defense as a cyber operations subject matter expert. His technical and operational expertise assisted in the stand-up of one of the first US Fleet Cyber Command/US 10th Fleet Cyber Mission Force teams. He continues to support DOD as a cyber operations SME.

Disclaimer

This book is strongly opinionated based on the experience of cybersecurity professionals with roughly 50 years combined between them and ranging across all categorical job functions and facets of the field. It is intended as an introspection regarding the body of work that is cybersecurity. It is also intended as a thought experiment to push those who read it toward a more theoretical approach to cybersecurity. By this, I mean not the theoretical conception of technologies that are used by cybersecurity professionals, but instead theoretical exploration of the craft itself.

Hard and sweeping issues within the field of cybersecurity will be identified, and hard questions posited in this book. Admittedly, a lot of answers will not be forthcoming. The reason for this is twofold. Firstly, answers can become dated, opinionated, and situational, so to avoid obsolescence, they will be brought up as concepts instead of detailed how-to's. As such, this book prefers to give the reader the ability to question and theory-craft in the cybersecurity domain rather than provide answers. Second, I like books that can be read front to back and have concepts that a reader walks away with, not a tool based how-to solution or operational guide that holds the reader's hand. Also, those books tend to be very heavy and long.

This is not to say that those types of text are not without their merit. For those breaking into the craft of cybersecurity they are great resources. This is instead aimed at those who have some experience in or are working with cybersecurity and aims to provide the basis for further theoretical exploration and introspection on cybersecurity.

DISCLAIMER

Much in this book may be contentious to some readers. We are all professionals with varying levels and areas of experience across the cybersecurity field as well as others. I encourage disagreement with points that may be made or explorations of cybersecurity contained herein. All I ask is that if you read a chapter or a topic and disagree with the point being made, you explore your argument defensibly and thoroughly. If after doing so, you arrive at a conclusion that what is written in this book is incorrect, I urge you to take the time to communicate that to other professionals as widely as possible so that the rest of the field may be the better for your own thought experiment of thoroughly contending what has been stated in the following chapters.

CHAPTER 1

Introduction

The motivation behind writing this book was the observed lack of theoretical cybersecurity in the field and the resulting gap in innovation, security, and cost-benefit. I have had the privilege several times in my maturing career within cybersecurity to be afforded the opportunity to serve in job functions where my role was largely to assess, evaluate, and postulate improvements to cybersecurity frameworks that mitigate risk for large organizations. This included both commercial Fortune 500 companies as well as government organizations with global enterprise and loss-of-life and mission-critical systems.

I often found myself talking with other senior cybersecurity professionals, including the other authors of this book, about why the field seems to lack good theoretics. In the following pages, I will attempt to do my best to outline and describe exactly what is meant by theoretical cybersecurity. Next, we will identify some foundational issues of the field that have led us to what is being described as the theoretical gap. Lastly, we will posit some thought experiments and theoretical concepts of our own.

What Is It?

Theoretical cybersecurity is the proposed branch of cybersecurity where abstractions of actual technologies, systems, and organizations are used to rationalize, explain, and innovate upon the body of work that is cybersecurity. Specifically, I mean toward the improvement of the trade, of the craft itself. As an analogy, consider early automobile manufacturing.

© Dr. Jacob G. Oakley, Michael Butler, Wayne York, Dr. Matthew Puckett, Dr. J. Louis Sewell 2022
J. G. Oakley et al., *Theoretical Cybersecurity*, https://doi.org/10.1007/978-1-4842-8300-4_1

The craft would be the designing and producing of automobiles. The technologies would be things such as riveters, welders, and paint guns. Improving the craft of automobile production involved the establishment of assembly lines. This is the type of improvement that I consider to be related to the craft rather than the technologies. I think in cybersecurity, we think we are doing a good enough job at innovation because we are constantly trying to one-up old technologies. Our field and those we protect would be the better for it if we also bettered and more often improved our craft itself.

It is also worth noting that good theoretical work is not just unadulterated and unbound pontification. Theoretical exploration of a craft should be rooted in the realistic constraints of the craft itself. This is not to limit the creativity of those doing the thinking. It is instead to ensure that when a theory is matured and ultimately experimented upon, the experiment is able to be designed in such a way as to prove out that the theory should be accepted as an improvement to the craft. Theoretical physicists, for instance, may think great and creative thoughts about the way things work at the macro or quantum levels. Their theories though must still be tied to the reality of their craft, in this case mathematics, such that when they conduct experiments on the theories, they are feasible, defensible as scientific proof. Otherwise, a theory could be posited, and an experiment created to prove or disprove it, but people may not necessarily believe the results to be true one way or another because there is too much detachment from reality. Once a theory has been proven, it can be taken by the applied physicists and become part of regular applications in the real world. Taking this back to a cybersecurity point, we need good theoretical cybersecurity that is both innovative as well as feasible enough to be proved out and make it to application across the broader field, or it is likely to be fruitless. Figure 1-1 shows out this process for theoretical cybersecurity, which is nothing different than many other scientific fields.

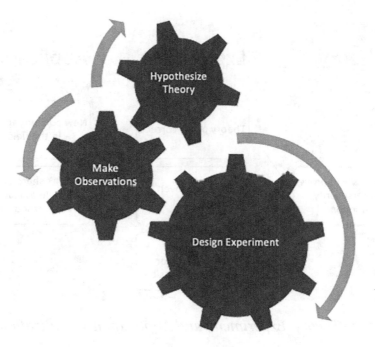

Figure 1-1. *Theoretical Cybersecurity Process*

Figure 1-2 shows the relationship between the theorization of a cybersecurity concept and its ultimate implications into the applied field.

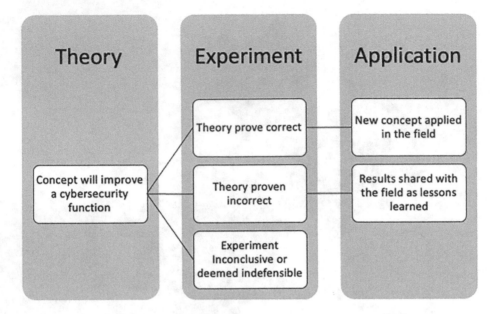

Figure 1-2. *Theory, Experiment, and Application Visualization*

It is vital that thought and experimentation is not wasted even when a concept is proven to be incorrect or is yet unproven. Disseminating knowledge of why a new theory was proven incorrect can still help inform the decision process of those professionals working regularly to apply known cybersecurity concepts. If an experiment was unable to prove a theory, this can act as a feedback loop for the theory itself and lend in refining the theory to a more provable state that is tied to reality.

What Is It Not?

Though the rest of the chapters will focus more on what theoretical cybersecurity can look like, why there isn't more of it, and so on, I think it is extremely useful to go through a case study of what it specifically is not. This is largely going to explore how important it is that the observation involved in leading to theoretical exploration of cybersecurity trade craft be informed by science and tempered by experience in the craft. In cybersecurity, the underlying science may be things such as mathematics or hard computer science. Unfortunately, when those sciences stray out of technological improvements and into trade craft discussions aimed at improving cybersecurity, the lack of experience and context can lead to a lot of wasted time and moot ideas.

Case Study

In general, theoretical work in any field is the application of the scientific method to support or reject a hypothesis. Though a bit of an oversimplification, this is true as well in cybersecurity. The foundational issue that I will illustrate next is that the scientific method must be applied by people who are not only capable of rigor and academic thought in the theorization and experimentation but also that are informed and experienced journeymen or masters of their craft. For instance, a mathematician with a bachelor's, master's, and PhD in math would certainly be considered a journeyman or master of the science of mathematics. In this case her craft is a science. On the other hand, someone with a bachelor's, master's, and PhD in cybersecurity, but no real-world experience, would assuredly not be considered a journeyman or master of her craft. In this example, the craft is cybersecurity, which requires a certain understanding of computer science and other scientific concepts to perform, but which is itself a craft rather than a science. This is in part due to some fundamental flaws in the way academia has approached cybersecurity as a cash cow more than a defensible pursuit, but more on that later.

More often than not, the folks attempting to theorize on cybersecurity concepts are academics with experience in computer science and other fields, but without a journeyman-level grasp on the body of work that is the field of cybersecurity. This leads to examples like the one I am about to walk through, and it is important to understand how the following differs from what will be prescribed later. The case study involved is indeed a theorization and an experimentation, but we must evaluate it through the lens of the craft and not just the technologies or, as you will see, we risk heavily investing in missteps. The following are not tied to any specific concept that has come forth but are close to several I have assessed in recent years. The case study does well to detail how attempts at innovation and theoretical cybersecurity can go awry.

Observation

Zero-day exploits give attackers a leg up on defenders because it allows them to come at defensive targets from previously unknown vectors. This makes it hard to be prepared for rapid pivoting, such as may be done by worms with a zero-day contained in them.

Theoretical Concept

To mitigate the impact of proliferated pivoting across an organization that is subject to an attacker leveraging a zero-day remote code execution vulnerability, systems should change constantly to make it harder for an attacker or an automated work to pivot around as the environment that is being attacked will constantly change. A changing attack surface to thwart malicious activity is known as a moving target defense or MTD. A way this could be done would be through randomly altering the ports used by certain services so that when an external entity throws an exploit against a port it sees, it is unlikely to succeed because the port is mapped to a different port on the host itself. Or the exploit may never get thrown because the attacker doesn't see the vulnerable service running because it is on an atypical port. Figure 1-3 shows how even in a linear network, where hosts can only be targeted after the attacker has gained access to the connected device, a zero-day-using worm can allow unfettered access.

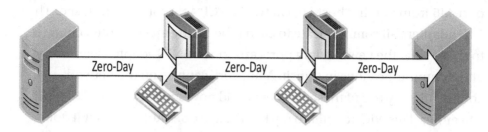

Figure 1-3. *Worm with Zero-Day*

This is representative of how the zero-day MS17-010 which targeted the Server Message Block version one protocol (SMBv1) and could have been used by a worm, such as it famously was in the Wannacry campaign, to exploit and pivot across machines running the vulnerable service on TCP port 445. Figure 1-4 shows this refined depiction of how a worm using MS17-010, which started as a completely unknown vulnerability, could pivot without pause since machines running SMBv1 on TCP port 445 had no idea they were vulnerable

Figure 1-4. *Worm with MS17-010*

Experiment

In our experiment, we will use a Network Interface Card (NIC) adapter that has been programmed to take ports listening on a local host and represent them to the rest of the network in a randomized fashion. This way to users on a given host, their processes are opening the expected ports. So, running a command to show what ports are listening on any of the below servers would show SMBv1 on TCP port 445, but if it were scanned on port 445 from another host on a network, TCP 445 would look closed. The NIC adapters all communicate to each other using an encrypted channel to share what the new random ports are and the NIC adapter seamlessly alters communications in transit. A network capture on the network connecting any two of these devices would now show traffic on TCP port 445 either. This NIC adapter to my knowledge does not exist, but it does well to give us a method for employing the MDT in our experiment, bear with me. Figure 1-5 shows how the ports for SMB would be represented on the network.

SMB on port 32403   SMB on port 21453   SMB on port 62031

Figure 1-5. *Randomized SMBv1 TCP Ports*

The experiment will involve having a scripted worm that tries to throw MS17-010 in across the linear network and attempt to pivot and re-throw the exploit to delve deeper into the network. So that the worm can act as if it is still leveraging a yet unknown zero-day, the machines involved will be running SMBv1 on port TCP 445 that is vulnerable to MS17-010. This would be run once without the NIC adapters as a control, and the results looked exactly like Figure 1-3. The worm exploited its way all the way to the server deepest in the network by throwing the SMBv1 exploit on port TCP 445 after scanning and finding it open. Next, the exploit is run against the same network, but with the MDT NIC adapter turned on, it presents an attack surface as shown in Figure 1-5 to the worm.

Results

Because the worm scanned to see if TCP 445 was open and then would throw the exploit at the target it was unable to pivot to a single machine. We can try to limit the worm less and have it thrown the exploit without scanning. In this case, it was thrown once from the attacker machine, but failed to gain access to the next machine because the worm threw MS17-010 on its known port of TCP 445, but the NIC Adapter presented SMBv1 to the network on TCP port 32403. The results are shown in Figure 1-6.

SMB on port 32403   SMB on port 21453   SMB on port 62031

Figure 1-6. *NIC Adapter Run 1*

Taking it a step further, we then make the network non-segmented to see if our MDT NIC Adapter is capable of providing the same protections in a network not also protected by segmentation. Figure 1-7 shows that even in this situation, the worm threw the MS17-010 zero-day exploit three times unsuccessfully because the SMBv1 protocol which was vulnerable is running on unexpected ports.

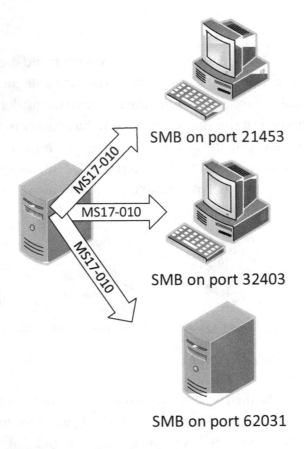

SMB on port 21453

MS17-010

MS17-010

MS17-010

SMB on port 32403

SMB on port 62031

Figure 1-7. *NIC Adapter Run 2*

Conclusions

Based on the results of this experiment, it is logical to conclude that the hypothesis that the cybersecurity technology concept involved in the moving target defense NIC Adapter was successful in stopping a worm that leverages a zero-day. This experiment can be scaled and repeated and provide the same results, traits that are a hallmark of good academic experimentation.

This experiment exercised the scientific method on a technology that implemented the conceptual theory of moving target defense in an example network. So, what is wrong with it? I will walk through dissecting this shortly, but at a very high level, this theory and experiment is computer science oriented and not cybersecurity oriented. I have no issue with this experiment or its results. I do see an issue with it being painted with the broad brush that has become cybersecurity. We get into dangerous waters when we use non-cybersecurity experiments and outcomes to make cybersecurity claims.

The title to the paper or grant application that might come as a result of this successful experimentation should probably be something as follows:

> *Preventing Automated Communication with TCP*
> *Port Randomization*

What I think it would actually be called to garner attention, funding, and aim at productization:

> *Preventing Zero-Day Attacks by APTs with Moving*
> *Target Defense*

The difference here is pretty clear, the latter title is definitely written with a cybersecurity lens applied. I think it is easy to say that using this experiment and the language of a title like that could allow our MDT NIC Adapter to be shown at a large cybersecurity conference as a product offered by a vendor. They would even run the simulation on a loop showing how the MDT NIC Adapter prevented an automated attack with a simulated zero-day over and over. Since the MDT NIC Adapter does not affect the host machine it connects to, there is no integration cost on a per host basis. Just unbox, plug in between the Ethernet and the machine, and sync the adapters across your network and Bam! You are protected from APTs and their worms with the academically proven protection of our MDT NIC Adapter.

Case Study Analysis

As was already mentioned, there is a foundational issue in this case study of using observation and experimentation that lacks the perspective of the actual craft of cybersecurity to make statements about how to better the craft through something like moving target defense. Now we will analyze the case study to detail the implications.

Cyber Sniff Test

Let's take a quick look at this whole case study through the craft side of the lens instead of purely scientific.

Observation and Theory

In our case study, the scientists made an observation that zero-days are problematic because the attack surface they target is not known ahead of time. This means that it is extremely difficult to prepare for. The novel thought that was had by the scientists was to hamper an unknown dynamic threat by presenting it with a dynamic and unknown attack surface. The theory is then that a dynamic attack surface via random port mapping with our MDT NIC Adapter on a networks host will slow down, if not wholly prevent, zero-day attacks and those that use them from pivoting around a network.

Nothing in the previous paragraph is factually inaccurate. Where it errs is a lack of context to inform the scientists on the reality of the problem they are theorizing at fixing. Let's walk through the actual type of threat this theory would be aimed at mitigating.

- It wouldn't stop external initial access such as would be established by phishing and other malware campaigns.

- It wouldn't stop an insider threat.

  - They would know of the technology and circumvent it.

  - If the MDT NIC was seamless, attacks launched from an insider computer would communicate without issue.

- It wouldn't stop an advanced persistent threat (APT) or even a less sophisticated human with interactive access.

  - They might have the context of an insider threat and those two points apply.

  - They would scan all ports and see that something odd was going on and work to circumvent it easily.

    - SMBv1 would still answer normally regardless of the TCP port it was communicating on, otherwise it couldn't function.

    - OS/Software fingerprinting available in free open source scans would likely catch this right off the bat.

- It won't stop an internet-based worm OUTSIDE the network using a zero-day because the remote hosts accessing internet facing resources won't all have access to something like the MDT NIC and therefore it can't run on internet facing attack surface or it would be problematic operationally.

- It might stop an automated attack such as a worm INSIDE the network with poor automation logic as it would fail as described in the experiment.

  - Though it is likely a tool deployed with a real zero-day was done by an interactive APT hacker who would notice its failed proliferation and adjust accordingly to circumvent it as mentioned earlier.

- It does not address less sophisticated actors that do not have zero-days for the same reasons.

Table 1-1. *Threats Prevented*

Origin	Vector	Prevented?
External	Phishing campaign	No
External	Worm using zero-day	No
External	APT using zero-day	No
External	Hacker using known exploit	No
Internal	Insider threat	No
Internal	APT using zero-day	No
Internal	Hacker using known exploit	No
Internal	Worm using known exploit	If it uses poor logic
Internal	Worm using zero-day	If it uses poor logic

In my opinion, the only realistic threat this would stop is an automated worm with bad automation logic, as is shown in Table 1-1. Zero-day exploits are extremely expensive, rare, and the first time they are used they are not nearly as effective, as the cat is likely to be out of the bag. This doesn't sound like the kind of resource that would be blindly deployed at all by sophisticated and nation state malicious actors, let alone via a worm with poor exploit logic.

Even if you disagree with some of my assumptions or conclusions, I think we can agree that in general, this observation and theory lack necessary context to be rooted in reality despite the supporting science. Further, the solution developed doesn't really have an existing problem to solve if you understand the way actual threats operate. This is a clear illustration of how science without cybersecurity context can lead to observations and theories that even if proved out such as ours was, don't lead to any meaningful contribution to the field.

Experimentation

Any experimentation to prove out theories and observations made from an inadequate perspective are bound to yield results that end up being of little value to the craft of cybersecurity. As we have just seen, they may prove out a theory and result in the successful marketing and dissemination of a tool or technology, but the likelihood that such a tool would actually mitigate cybersecurity risk are low or coincidental. Later in this book, we will spend an entire chapter on designing good cybersecurity experiments, but first we will cover what it will take for the field to begin generating more theoretical cybersecurity paradigms.

Implications for Implementation

One last thing I will cover in a small amount here and which will be covered later is how there is a distinct need for understanding implications and true cost benefit. Whether observation, theory, and experimentation are done purely scientifically or with context of the craft, implications of advertised cost benefit are not often sufficiently incorporated into evaluating true cost benefit. Even if we thought our MDT NIC Adapter provided improved mitigation, we need to take it many steps further in understanding the cost benefit of such a technology.

One quick set of examples would be the downstream implications to other cybersecurity apparatus post implementation. Our MDT NIC adapter randomizes exposed TCP ports, and the traffic will travel to the new random ports between hosts. This means that any network-based intrusion detection system (IDS) or security information and event management software (SEIM) won't be able to leverage their heuristics or other capabilities because the traffic will look odd to them too. Further, actions such as forensics activities and threat hunting will also be hampered by having to tie what was captured or seen on the network with logs of what was the state of the MDT randomization at the time of other events.

With just these quickly mentioned implications to putting in place even an MDT NIC Adapter that did provide actual security mitigation, is it likely to do so to the extent that it is worth addressing the other sunk costs and movement of risk and work across the attack surface? I think not. This is not always the answer, but this is the bare minimum extent to which implications must be taken into consideration, even for valid theories and concepts, when we evaluate the cost benefit of a novel cybersecurity idea. In a later chapter, we will deep dive on understanding and evaluating true cost benefit in cybersecurity. This is an integral part of the craft, this is the way.

Summary

We have touched on the concept of theoretical cybersecurity and walked through a detailed case study to really hit home what is meant. The typical academic and industry scientific theorization and experimentation are not what I would call theoretical cybersecurity, they are more exploration of a particular science involved in information technology. We have discussed that what is most important in cybersecurity in general and its theoretical endeavors specifically is that it is a field which requires a strong scientific understanding of various technologies and concepts as a starting point, but which should be measured largely based on experience in the craft. The case study was used to show the separation between science and craft from a theorization perspective and how it leads to consequential impacts to the field in general.

It could be argued that if theoretical cybersecurity were only performed with a journeyman type of perspective, many potential academic achievements and innovations may be missed as thus limits the researcher population. Perhaps, the preceding case study leads to some other finding that ends up benefiting the field. That is more than fine, and I hope it does. What I am shouting from a soap box to the industry is that such an example is not theoretical cybersecurity and that we need more of what I have deemed theoretical cybersecurity if we are going to achieve meaningful improvements to our craft that aren't. As we will see in the coming chapters, it is hard to get the right people to make the observations and come up with theories, and it is hard to come up with good cybersecurity experimentation because when it is done right, it requires science and a lot of human involvement, which makes defensibility challenging. Most importantly, much of what is yet to be covered focuses on understanding, providing, and ensuring cost benefit as an outcome of cybersecurity, which should always be evaluated through the amount of cybersecurity risk mitigation necessary to secure strategic objectives of any organization.

CHAPTER 2

A Cyber Taxonomy

As we analyzed the example in the previous chapter, it becomes apparent
that there is inherently a problem with the outcomes of research when
it is done by people with the wrong context, knowledge experience, or
backgrounds. In this chapter, we will explore what sort of people make the
right choice when theoretical cybersecurity work, thought, and innovation
are necessary. First though, we need to address the taxonomical issue that
is plaguing the cybersecurity industry and is at least in part responsible for
more widespread issues. If we can understand what the problems are with
the way we classify professionals in cybersecurity, we can better find the
right people to employ in theoretical exploration of new concepts.

A Case of Identity Crisis

What is cybersecurity? Who is a cybersecurity professional? Those are
tough questions; I will cede to a major manifester for some defensible
definition.

Officially, in the US federal government, the term was defined on
January 8, 2008, in National Security Presidential Directive/NSPD-54 and
Homeland Security Presidential Directive/HSPD-23 as

> Cybersecurity means prevention of damage to,
> protection of, and restoration of computers,
> electronic communications systems, electronic
> communication services, wire communication, and

electronic communication, including information
contained therein, to ensure its availability
integrity, authentication, confidentiality, and non-
repudiation.

This document and others related to it as well as to cybersecurity
rolled out across the United States. This led to a lot of things, such as the
formation of U.S. CYBERCOM, it also led to an immense amount of federal
funding getting tied to the terms cyber and cybersecurity. Anecdotally,
what happened next was that contracts started having such terms in them
and so did requests for proposals, proposals themselves, and the products,
services, and people associated with such documents. In furtherance
of this, the Department of Defense (DoD), in March of 2014, formally
changed any use of the term Information Assurance to cybersecurity. I
only pick on the DoD specifically because we will use their taxonomy as a
point of understanding before working toward our own. So, I guess in the
abstract, we can blame the US government and money associated with its
budgets and contracts for the diluted and overextended nature of the term
cybersecurity.

Let us look at a couple example job titles that are great at illustrating
how this has played out, cybersecurity analyst and cybersecurity engineer.
If you were to do a job search on these terms on any popular site, you
would find they can mean quite different things in different places.

Cybersecurity Analyst

So, what types of jobs might a cybersecurity analyst do? Here is a quick list
off the top of my head:

- Intelligence Analysis

- Network Analysis

- Vulnerability Analysis

- Security Operations Center (SOC) Analyst

- Risk Analyst

- Compliance Auditor

- Compliance Manager

- Hunt Team Operator

- Red Team Operator

- Penetration Tester

- Forensics Analyst

Now, if we just used those terms, we would readily understand a good deal about the job functions associated with that given analyst role. Instead, since there is so much money behind the term cybersecurity in government, academia, and industry, we use a singular term that significantly muddies the water.

Cybersecurity Engineer

Now let us look at cybersecurity engineer; this is almost worse to me because it also abuses the term engineer, and usually toward the specific goal of charging more for the person in the billet. The following is my off-the-cuff list of all the different things a cybersecurity engineer might actually be:

- Cloud Administrator

- Network Administrator

- Systems Administrator

- Domain Administrator

- Firewall Administrator

- Security Operations Center (SOC) Analyst

- Compliance Auditor

- Compliance Manager

- Hunt Team Operator

- Red Team Operator

- Penetration Tester

As with the cybersecurity analyst, the term cybersecurity and engineer have both been made so ambiguous as to become almost completely useless in describing something. Yet, the money in the industry has driven the terminology.

Comparison

Now, let's just compare those two, already ultra-ambiguous terms and we can see that they even share many of the same types of job functions. These are not the only job titles that have grown tremendous ambiguity thanks to where cybersecurity terminology has led us, but they are certainly the most illustrative of the problem.

As you can see after reviewing Table 2-1, six of the roles could be either a cybersecurity analyst or engineer. This means that over half of the ones I thought easily associated with either term could be advertised under either job name.

Table 2-1. *Comparison of Roles and Responsibilities*

Roles	Title: Cybersecurity analyst	Title: Cybersecurity engineer
Intelligence analysis	YES	NO
Network Analysis	YES	NO
Vulnerability Analysis	YES	NO
SOC Analyst	**YES**	**YES**
Risk Analyst	YES	NO
Compliance Auditor	**YES**	**YES**
Compliance Manager	**YES**	**YES**
Hunt Team Operator	**YES**	**YES**
Red Team Operator	**YES**	**YES**
Penetration Tester	**YES**	**YES**
Forensics Analyst	YES	NO
Cloud Administrator	NO	YES
Network Administrator	NO	YES
Systems Administrator	NO	YES
Domain Administrator	NO	YES
Firewall Administrator	NO	YES

Taxonomy of the Profession

In Figure 2-1, which is available at `https://public.cyber.mil/cw/dcwf/`, we can see what the United States DoD thinks a good taxonomy is of various cyber roles. I am including to show a known taxonomy and we will move past it into our own taxonomy. This is partially due to the military nature of the DoD one, as well as some of the roles not meshing well with the wider cybersecurity industry that we are discussing in this book.

Analyze
Performs highly-specialized review and evaluation of incoming cybersecurity information to determine its usefulness for intelligence.

Collect & Operate
Provides specialized denial and deception operations and collection of cybersecurity information that may be used to develop intelligence.

Investigate
Investigates cybersecurity events or crimes related to information technology (IT) systems, networks, and digital evidence.

Operate & Maintain
Provides the support, administration, and maintenance necessary to ensure effective and efficient information technology (IT) system performance and security.

Oversee & Govern
Provides leadership, management, direction, or development and advocacy so the organization may effectively conduct cybersecurity work.

Protect & Defend
Identifies, analyzes, and mitigates threats to internal information technology (IT) systems and/or networks.

Securely Provision
Conceptualizes, designs, procures, and/or builds secure information technology (IT) systems, with responsibility for aspects of system and/or network development.

Figure 2-1. *DoD Taxonomy*

As I mentioned, we will not have in out taxonomy that will be leverage for the rest of this book the analyze, collect and operate roles in the same way or at all as they are a foreign intelligence gathering, act of war type of activity that specifically falls under US Code Title 10 and Title 50.

Further, I think this a good point to address one function that will be missing from our taxonomy and that is programmers, coders, or developers. These functions do have security considerations to their own craft such as secure coding in general and DevSecOps specifically. These are activities though that fall under the craft of those individuals and is not in my mind a cybersecurity function. Further, security issues that are potentially introduced via poor practices of such professionals already have cybersecurity functions associated with the identification and mitigation of such cybersecurity risk.

Our Taxonomy

If in the end you decide that you like the DoD taxonomy or some other taxonomy better or find them more accurate, that is of course fine and well. For the purpose of follow-on discussion though, you will want to refer to the one we will outline in this chapter as further work builds on the foundational point being made and less the specificity of one given category of roles and responsibilities over another.

Types of Cybersecurity

In the following, I will describe the eight types of cybersecurity roles that I will use in our taxonomy and that will be referenced in later chapters. I make no claim that this is perfect or the most accurate specific to a given situation; it is simply the best structure I could come up with to make my point about theoretical cybersecurity and who should really be doing it. If you prefer your own taxonomy of roles or functions, then I suspect you could leverage it in a way similar to how we will at the end of this chapter. Our taxonomy is shown in Figure 2-2 and described in the following section.

Figure 2-2. *Our Taxanomy*

Detect

By detective roles, we mean any that are involved in the aggregation and analysis of data about a system to perform work in a detect function. The following is a list of examples (not comprehensive) that could fall within this cybersecurity role:

- Net flow and other SOC-related analysis

- Intrusion detection system analysis

- Behavior analytics analysis

Investigate

Investigative roles are those that not only analyze aggregated data provided by other systems, products, and software but also key off of such data and go exploring or hunting to actively collect related data from systems and logs. The main delimiter between detective and investigative at an extremely abstract level is the active nature of investigation in a cybersecurity sense compared to detective. The following are examples of job roles with an investigative function:

- Threat hunting operations

- Forensics analysis

- Blue team type analysis such as nmap scanning

Create

In the create role, we are talking about those individuals involved in the creation of the infrastructure that run a given organization or network. They are responsible for setting up the systems in a secure manner as well as designing them to support operational needs and security requirements. One key attribute of create roles is that they are not directly interfacing with the eventual users of a system. Instead, they are responsible for building the system or sections of it. It is also important to address here the lack of programmers and developers from our taxonomy. Even with the growing prevalence of secure development operations in the form of things like DevSecOps, there may be utilization by the developers at various stages of their pipeline. This does not mean that they are responsible for cybersecurity considerations. I think it is important to involve security early on in such processes by leveraging things like static and dynamic code analysis tools, but for similar reasons to our moving defense example, relying on people too far from real cybersecurity perspective to have appropriate context can't be dangerous. Therefore, our create role will not include people who interface with systems at the code commit role, as their primary responsibility is that a system perform the actions it was written for and security is traditionally secondary. Example jobs with this role are as follows:

- Router administrator

- Network designer

- Firewall administrator

Operate

The operate role covers those that maintain, repair, and operate the software and settings that run on a system. Unlike the create role, those performing operate actions are often interfacing with the users of the system as well. This brings about a unique cybersecurity challenge to the operate role over the create role in that the most vulnerable part of a system (the people who use it) is the major reason for operate roles to perform their actions. Example jobs that perform the operate role are as follows:

- Helpdesk technician

- Domain administrator

- Website administrator

Architect

The architect role is that which designs cybersecurity systems, policies, and procedures with varying degrees of diversity. A job which I am not indicating falls within this role, and the one which falls more within the journeyman concept, which we will cover later this chapter, is that of cybersecurity architect. A cybersecurity architect is responsible for designing the cybersecurity architecture an organization will use to mitigate risk and enable strategic outcomes. This involves knowledge of and design to every facet of cybersecurity as a body of work. Different than this are role-specific architects who are responsible for designing the implementation of a portion of the larger cybersecurity architecture. Examples of these architect roles, which represent this role of designing specific facets within cybersecurity, are as follows:

- Network architect

- Cloud architect

- Software solution architect

Audit

The audit role is that of compliance, verification, and validation. In this role, individuals are responsible for ensuring that policies, regulations, and standards are being followed and implemented in a system. This can be from the cybersecurity perspective of the organization that owns the system, or it can be by and for a regulatory body that governs the organization actions. In the Department of Defense, this could be system accreditation under NIST RMF, or in the financial industry or healthcare, it could be SEC or HIPAA regulations, respectively. Examples of this role are listed next. In this role, we will also place those that manage the policies and certain auditable assets as the skillsets are nearly identical.

- Compliance engineer/manager

- Compliance auditors

- Independent verification and validation teams

Analyze

Analysis is a term thrown around the entirety of the cybersecurity industry and community, as I indicated in the example where I compared cybersecurity analyst and engineer job titles. In our taxonomy though, we are using it to describe the role of those who make assessments and analysis on data that was not collected or produced purposefully by the hardware and software in a network. That fact is what delimits this role from something like a SOC analyst who is reviewing logs and events and data created by the system's devices. This is more an intelligence creation and analysis role performed by assessing more abstract information about a system and its cybersecurity such as network maps, user behavior, threat data, and so on, and examples are listed as follows:

- Threat intelligence

- Open source intelligence analyst

- Vulnerability analyst

- Exploitation or targeting analyst

Emulate

The last role I will cover is that of emulation. This is where the various levels of adversarial emulation are performed to test, assess, and exercise the cybersecurity apparatus of an organization. This can lead not only to remediation and further mitigation of discovered issues but also to allow defensive mechanisms to be tested and validated through response to the emulation. Job that would perform this role are as follows:

- Web application penetration tester

- Network penetration tester

- Red team operator

Functional Subsets

Next, we will add to our taxonomy by dividing the eight roles we have covered into four functional subsets that tie together somewhat similar experience, knowledge, and skills needed to perform the activities in such job roles. Figure 2-3 shows the four functional areas and the roles they encompass.

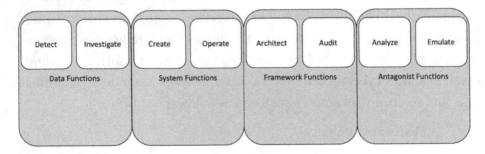

Figure 2-3. *Functional Subsets*

Data Functions

Job roles that have a data function are those that require data about the system, from the system to be performed. Both detective and investigative job roles require a cybersecurity professional to be versed in analyzing information that systems produce. Though the data may be collected somewhat passively in the case of detect roles and active for investigative roles, the perspective that such information is analyzed from is very similar.

System Functions

While there is a difference in job roles that are customer- or user-facing and those that are not, the job roles that perform system functions rely on similar actions by cybersecurity professionals. Diagnosis of issues may differ when users or customers are involved, but configuring, setting up, and fixing systems are done by similarly experienced roles requiring a similar skillset. Job roles in the system's functional domain require understanding of command line syntax, underlying infrastructure, and overall configuration of the devices that make up a system.

Framework Functions

Architecture roles create frameworks, and auditing roles evaluate, verify, and validate them. In either case, there is a need to have an in-depth understanding of what a framework is intended to accomplish, why it has been put in place, and how it is intended to function. As such, both types of cybersecurity job roles can be lumped into a framework function group.

Antagonist Functions

Antagonist functions are those that require an antagonistic or adversarial perspective and understanding to best perform the cybersecurity role. This is obviously the case with emulation roles such as red teaming or penetration testing. It is also required when performing intelligence analysis of an organization or system. This is because instead of making analysis of system-created or system-collected data, the assessment and analysis focus on information related to the scoping and targeting of an organization with the specific fact that motivation is antagonistic in nature.

Actional Subsets

It is also worth showing the roles in our taxonomy based on the split between roles involving reactive and proactive cybersecurity. Figure 2-4 shows this delineation.

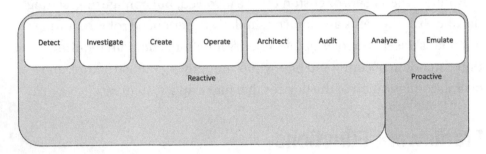

| Detect | Investigate | Create | Operate | Architect | Audit | Analyze | Emulate |

Reactive   Proactive

Figure 2-4.

Reactive

The majority of cybersecurity roles are reactive in that they require information from existing attacks to inform security functions. Even threat hunting, which is often referred to as generally proactive, requires knowledge of actors, associations, or other attributions to inform hunt activity.

Proactive

Emulate job roles are mostly proactive as they rely on individuals to attack a system as a malicious actor would. This attempt to discover misconfigurations and new exploitation efforts make it proactive. In the same way that threat hunting is not truly proactive, there are times when unsophisticated penetration testing can also be viewed this way. When performed by less skilled individuals or with certain motivations in respect to time and scope, scanning and exploitation of only known capabilities is also arguably not proactive. The reason the proactive domain extends partially into the analyze role is that there are times where intelligence assessments made about threats or systems can provide truly proactive information to guide cybersecurity efforts.

Analogy

Now that we have covered our taxonomy that will be leveraged for this chapter and others, we will show an analogy of similar roles in a different industry. This should aid to illustrate the point we are making at the end of this chapter regarding the professionals most appropriate for theoretical cybersecurity endeavors. We will call this industry in our analogy the shopping mall industry. The goal of the shopping mall industry is for its malls to stay open and operational as long as possible. Figure 2-5 shows the taxonomy of job roles for our mall operations and what follows is a quick list of these roles with descriptions.

Figure 2-5.

Detective

Our shopping mall industry detective work, where data is gathered from systems in the shopping mall, could include many types of detective data analytics that support shopping mall operations. These analytics could be based on detecting data from things like security cameras, HVAC systems, power usage, and others that can allow shopping mall operators to tailor the usage of these systems to optimize longevity of business operations.

Investigative

For an investigative analogy in the shopping mall business, we will put pest control professionals in this role as they go through and look for things like termites and other pests that might impact the structural integrity of the mall or impact business operations.

Create

For the create role, we will refer to those that built the shopping malls including carpenters, plumbers, electricians, and others.

Operate

For the operate role, we will have those professionals in the shopping mall industry that interface with the customers and users of the mall. This could be repairmen, retail staff of shops in the mall, cleaning crews, and others that keep the mall operational.

Architects

Here architects will be those structural architects who designed the mall. We don't have the same need to separate these architects from broader architects as shopping mall operations architecture is not a thing.

Auditors

Shopping mall operations also have auditors who ensure that mall policies are kept up as well as other regulations and standards are followed. This could include things like workplace safety standards auditing by an organization like OSHA or a fire marshal making sure that stores are not over capacity.

Intelligence Creators

Just as intelligencer assessments can inform cybersecurity activities, shopping malls can have business-related intelligence. Business intelligence can be about where to place what types of stores in the mall based on purchasing habits for instance.

Adversary Emulation

Adversary emulation for a shopping mall is a little less likely than this job role is in cybersecurity; however, a shopping mall operator could certainly hire physical penetration testers to see how easy it is to do things like shoplift or break into the mall given its security system and cameras.

So, What's the Point?

The thesis of this chapter is that we need to identify the right type of people to perform theoretical cybersecurity efforts for the betterment of the industry and to improve the body of work. The reason for this shopping mall taxonomy is to illustrate the importance and relevance of our suggested theoretical cybersecurity professionals. In shopping mall operations, individuals would need varied and lengthy experience across several job roles to realistically provide contextual and defensible theoretical improvements to shopping malls.

Someone with time spent as a retail professional and as a builder of malls or as a business intelligence professional would have a wealth of perspective and experience to draw from. The importance of this context, as discussed in Chapter 1, is that it allows for theoretical ideas to be framed by reality, in this case the reality of operating a shopping mall. The opposite is also true that experience in only one facet of shopping mall operations would not make someone reasonably capable of coming up with theoretical shopping mall ideas.

The Tradecraft Concepts

The same concepts are true of cybersecurity as well, that variance and depth of experience across the body of work is necessary to produce professionals with the appropriate context to explore theoretical cybersecurity. Our shopping mall analogy is useful to make at least two points regarding cybersecurity professionals. First, to further my point about developers not being cybersecurity professionals. In the same way that the developers of a point-of-sale machine do not need to have in-depth knowledge of shopping mall operations, neither do developers of code need in-depth knowledge of cybersecurity. Second, our scientists from Chapter 1, who came up with the moving target idea without good cybersecurity context, are a lot like the scientists who design better nails through metallurgy or plastic flooring through chemistry but would not be expected to conduct experiments toward shopping mall operations.

This isn't to say that things like better nails and better flooring through scientific experimentation aren't necessary and beneficial because they are. The point is that they do not perform experiments on their areas of expertise in chemistry or metallurgy and call it a shopping mall experiment. This is essentially what happened with our Chapter 1 example. Scientists who are experienced in something such as computer science performed a computer science experiment and billed it as a result that proved a cybersecurity concept.

So how do we avoid this? How do we insure that the people carrying out theoretical exploration in the field of cybersecurity are doing so with the right context and experience behind their efforts to result in true cybersecurity innovation?

What we propose is a sort of tradecraft structure where individuals in the functional areas we outlined in our earlier taxonomy represent four domains of cybersecurity apprenticeship. In a specific functional area, we could say that two years make an apprentice, six years make a journeyman, and ten years make a master. Years of experience could also count as years in completing a relevant bachelor's or master's degree. These timelines are similar to other trades such as electricians and plumbers. We can then levy this system to create apprentices, journeymen, and masters within the broader body of cybersecurity.

We could say that once a person has six years of experience in a functional domain (becoming a journeyman in that domain) they are an apprentice of cybersecurity at the broader stage. To become a journeyman of cybersecurity though, we should require someone to be a journeyman in one domain and at least an apprentice in another. Further, we could say a master cybersecurity practitioner must be a master of a domain and at least an apprentice in another or be a journeyman of two different functional domains. Figure 2-6 shows this example structure.

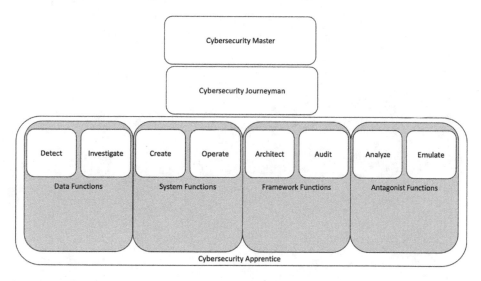

Figure 2-6. *Cybersecurity Trade Levels*

Summary

To wrap up, we have established a trade structure for the cybersecurity tradecraft. The semantics of our system bear hashing out at scale and the years of experience and other requirements could certainly be put up for debate. The takeaway is that we should establish some structure that produces a minimum qualification for professionals in cybersecurity to be considered journeymen or masters of the trade and not of specific functional domains. If we can do that as a field, we will have a pool of professionals who could be entrusted to take the lead and provide direction for further theoretical cybersecurity.

CHAPTER 3

Cost Benefit

In this chapter, we will explore the concept of cost benefit and how it applies within the cybersecurity industry. The term itself is rather self-descriptive. Cost benefit is an assessment of how beneficial something is when offset with cost. Typically, the benefit in cost benefit, when referred to in cybersecurity constructs, is the ability to mitigate risk. Risk could be risk of exploitation or other worries, but they all roll up to either financial risk or loss of life or both. Typically, the cost in cost benefit, when the term is referred to in cybersecurity circles, is a cost in dollars, but this does not necessarily have to be the case; sometimes, it could be in the form of resources or time spent, but ultimately, those too get rolled up into a dollar amount.

Good cybersecurity cost benefit is when you implement a cybersecurity product, capability, or subscribe to a cybersecurity service that mitigates enough cybersecurity induced that the cost of that asset is positively offset by the risk it mitigates. Bad cost benefit is when the cost of the asset far outstrips the potential benefit that could be gained from implementation. There are many defensible ways to metric cost and benefit and a dearth of calculative ways to determine whether a given cost benefit is good or bad. That is not the focus of cost benefit in this chapter or book. Instead, the takeaway is hopefully that you as the reader are able to assess cost benefit in your own terms, situationally, and as needed, but in a way that explores not just what a product, service, or capability aims to provide but whether in doing so it truly provides cost benefit at the strategic, organizational level.

Being able to appropriately determine cost benefit is the difference between being able to convince people or not that they should buy or use your cybersecurity thing. It is also the difference between procuring and implementing cybersecurity things that benefit your organization or not. Even in cybersecurity, it is all about sales, and selling in our case involves (or should anyway) proving true cost benefit of cybersecurity.

There is admittedly a slight difference in selling cost benefit between commercial and regulated spaces such as the DoD, HIPAA, or financial institutions. In commercial environments, you have to sell people (your boss, their boss, shareholders) on cybersecurity itself by using the best combination of products, capabilities, and services you can architect together. In regulated spaces, cybersecurity itself is required, so you are instead in the position of having to illustrate the cost benefit of a given product, service, or capability within the defined architecture the organization is already being held to such as the risk management framework (RMF) put out by the National Institute of Standards and Technology (NIST).

For the sake of brevity, I will start using the term cybersecurity thing, which is intended to represent a cybersecurity product, capability, or service. When we consider the cost benefit of a cybersecurity thing, we first need to ask five simple questions that may have very complex answers:

1. What is the intended specific technical cost benefit?

2. Does that specific cost benefit translate into organization-wide cybersecurity cost benefit?

3. Does that cybersecurity cost benefit translate into strategic cost benefit?

4. How long or at what point does it become cost beneficial?

5. How long does the cost benefit last?

Warning

I am about to make some statements that may been seen as contentious; you may not agree with them. If you do not agree with the following statement, I hope you read on and give me a chance to prove my point to you and outline exactly what I mean.

No one cares about cybersecurity.

There, I said it. I suppose we could clarify and say that specifically, cybersecurity vendors and cybersecurity consumers don't care about cybersecurity. The professionals on both sides of the producer consumer equation are often passionate about cybersecurity and enjoy the puzzling, problem-solving nature of the body of work we are a part of. Being blunt though, until we as cybersecurity professionals truly understand what really drives cybersecurity-related decisions by vendors and consumers, we will not be able to help them be secure despite themselves.

That statement is probably not going to make me a lot of friends among future cybersecurity employers, but let's get into the what and why of such an audacious statement.

Real Motivation

All right, so we have covered what is meant by cybersecurity cost benefit and that it is important when trying to offer or consume a cybersecurity thing. The next concept that needs to be understood before we talk about applying the good cost benefit analysis to cybersecurity things is a harsh reality, an ugly truth or whatever other label you want to give to what I just said.

No matter the lip service of any government institution or commercial organization, they really don't care about cybersecurity. They care about their own strategic goals, objectives, and outcomes. Sure, cybersecurity is seen as either a challenge to or a protector of those strategic outcomes, but no organization actually has cybersecurity as a strategic outcome. If you are the Department of Defense, you are trying to save lives and protect the country, having good cybersecurity helps you make sure you can do that in contested environments like the cyber domain.

If you are a vendor like, you may provide cybersecurity to an organization like the Department of Defense, but your strategic outcome is to make money and continue your existence. Unlike those federally funded research and development centers (FFRDCs) or not-for-profit organizations like MITRE, you are still beholden to budgets to pay your employees and without focusing on that foremost the people running such organizations still risk them folding. This is not to say that vendor organizations' best path to achieving their strategic outcome isn't providing good cybersecurity for their consumers, I am just trying to get everyone to acknowledge that no organization has cybersecurity as a strategic outcome, and strategic outcomes drive cost benefit.

Examples

If you still disagree with me about my abhorrent statement about no one caring about cybersecurity I have some illustrative examples of this being the case that span the gamut of cybersecurity industry functional domains.

Industry Wide Example: Retention

This one is a pet peeve of mine, so I apologize for the tower of soap boxes we currently sit atop. It is my opinion that complaining about retention in the cybersecurity industry is obnoxious. I hear and see things like, "Well every time I train up a person or they get certified or finish their degree they move on to another position." Then you as the employer didn't try hard enough to retain them. I would think that if you took that person's new resume, and had it sent as an applicant to replace the person who you just let go, they would probably get about the same pay as that person is getting at their new place of employment. Worse, you've lost the tribal knowledge that person has about the security apparatus they work within in addition to their technical skills and experience.

My main point though is not that I get annoyed about companies complaining about a retention problem they could solve themselves by promoting within and rewarding organic growth. The point to illustrate is that such companies (most if we are honest) show they don't care about cybersecurity because they let the tribal knowledge walk. It is worse, or maybe I am just more familiar with government contracting, but the story goes something like this:

1. Leverage the resumes of talented people to win a contract.

2. Hire as cheap of resources as possible to staff contract personnel requirements.

3. If they grow through certification or degrees of years of experience and want more salary, let them find other employment.

4. Hire the cheapest person possible to fill the same slot and bill the same rate to maximize profits.

5. It doesn't matter if they do well, the government is incentivized to pick a new contractor on re-compete anyways, so they don't look like they are playing favorites. They are also incentivized to spend all the money they set aside for that contract otherwise they can lose budget allocations for follow-on years. The work would have to be so poor that it became worth the government's time to kick the company off and re-allocate the funds, and that is almost never going to happen.

OK, that was a bit extreme, and maybe jaded. However, when cybersecurity vendors let contract positions become vacant instead of re-investing in their people, they are often doing so to maximize the profitability of that contract. Conversely, if they had the cybersecurity of their customer as a strategic outcome (which they don't, they are a business) they would ensure the tribal knowledge that would provide greater cybersecurity from such personnel stayed on the contract. It is not malicious or wrong for a cybersecurity vendor to have profitability as a strategic outcome and not cybersecurity. However, it is important as we evaluate where the cybersecurity industry is at for us to acknowledge this as a truth.

Defensive Cybersecurity Example: Metrics

If you have ever been a member of a security operations center (SOC) where detect functions are executed to provide cybersecurity, you may already know the point here. In many SOCs, it is more about cybersecurity theater than it is about providing actual cybersecurity. This is because in the best SOC, operated perfectly and run with the best tools, signatures, and by the best professionals in the most secure network, you would probably never get an alert.

I can tell you from personal experience it is very hard to continue to prove the cost benefit of nothing. So how do we try and communicate the value of our SOC to the people paying for it. The most common example I have seen is reporting metrics that sound impressive but have little to no cybersecurity meaning. Every reporting period, the SOC says it had some million number of events monitored, and they saw some hundreds of thousands of hits on their external firewall. Well, all those statements mean that their publicly accesible attack surface is constantly getting scanned and probed by countless Internet-based agents just like every other Internet IP and that they have a large network that produces lots of events. To an operations- or business-focused person though, that sounds like they are doing a lot of work.

Again, if we are honest, the professionals who set up, operate, and maintain the SOC may very well care about cybersecurity. The SOC provider cares about maintaining the SOC contract and the customer cares about checking a box that they have a SOC so they cover their butts. The cheaper the better as long as they can keep telling their boss that the SOC has millions of events covered and hundreds of thousands of firewall hits monitored. Even in organic settings where a company stands up its own SOC, the person who is in charge of the SOC personnel still wants to keep his or her team the same size or grow it, and wants to keep their job and insure their people's jobs.

Offensive Cybersecurity Example: Reporting

The last example I would like to bring up is the one I am most familiar with and which I speak about in my book Professional Red Teaming. There are countless times where an offensive cybersecurity event is carried out and the end results are ignored, thrown out, or destroyed. This is done for several reasons. The customer, if they are the head of IT or security, for example, may not have the funds to fix anything in the report and knows they won't get them even with the report as evidence. So, they have the assessment conducted so they can tell their boss they did it or check a compliance box and then they throw away the liability that is an offensive security assessment.

The example I use in my other book is, imagine a hospital gets an offensive cybersecurity assessment done and there are ten findings. Say they do have funds to fix everything, but it will take a three-year period to cover all ten remediations, so they prioritize them and get to work securing their network. Now, a little over a year in, they have remediated four of the ten findings and are working on the fifth when an attacker leverages finding six to get into their network and steal HIPAA data for their patients. One of the patients sues the hospital and subpoenas their security-related documents, which include the report from a year ago with the ten findings.

Imagine the optics in the court room when they say, "look you all knew about this vulnerability for over a year, and it was in a report you got from a security team and now it was used to compromise my clients' data."

Pretty bad optics, right? Probably a case the hospital loses I'd guess. It is situations like this that drive people to pay for such assessments so they can say they did their due diligence but often the findings are a liability for any number of reasons. Again, if we are honest, the ethical hackers may actually care about the cybersecurity of the hospital. The hospital itself cares about protecting its financial interests and the offensive security vendor cares about keeping its professionals employed and expanding its customer base. The great cybersecurity professionals are the ones that find ways to help make the hospital more secure within the constraints of neither the vendor they work for nor the hospital actually having cybersecurity as their strategic outcome.

Understanding Cost Benefit Perspectives

We have covered at a high level what cost benefit means and how the term applies within the cybersecurity industry. What I would like to do now is to show that within cybersecurity there are different ways of evaluating cost benefit depending on the perspective involved. It is essential to understand how cost benefit is evaluated by all those involved in cybersecurity to come up with truly appropriate evaluations of cost benefit.

Cost Benefit to the Target

The more familiar perspective for most of us when considering cost benefit is to do so as the target of potential attack. In this perspective, the focus is on the perceived value of various aspects of the organization and how much should be spent to burn down risk to those assets. In our case, we are talking about burning down cybersecurity-related risks to such assets.

Consider a credit bureau as our target. There are several major entities; I will not pick a specific one, so let's just call them TransExperiafax. Now, though TransExperiafax offers credit reporting, monitoring, and protection to the people whose credit files they keep, most of their money is made from data analytics based on the files they keep. Let's say Transexperiafax makes an annual revenue of 2.5 billion from selling their data analytics to other companies. Also, they were recently the victim of a cybersecurity breach, and when it was announced, they lost 10% of their stock market cap, which equated to a 1-billion-dollar loss for the year for their shareholders.

If we think about how TransExperiafax might evaluate cost benefit itself as a potential target of future attacks, those two values are probably key. The 2.5 billion annually and 1 billion due to a breach are likely to be the strategic cost benchmarks to determine how much they are willing to spend on cybersecurity efforts toward protecting those year-over-year values and mitigating or avoiding catastrophic events.

Using these numbers, maybe TransExperiafax decides they'll spend 1% of the 2.5 billion annual risk plus the 1 billion potential loss values, each year, spread over 12 months equally. Their cybersecurity spending would look like Figure 3-1.

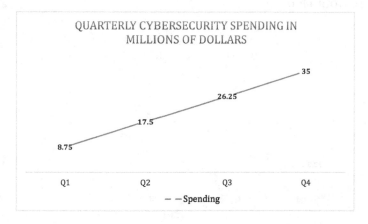

Figure 3-1. *Target Cost Benefit*

Cost Benefit to the Attacker

Unfortunately for TransExperiafax, the enemy gets a vote on cost benefit too. At least, they will have their own way of evaluating it. In what way does the attacker evaluate cost benefit? The easiest way for us to consider this is to make an assumption (probably a fair one) that the most likely malicious actor to target TransExperiafax is going to be an organized crime activity, potentially somehow tied to a foreign government, but not necessarily. If this is the case, then they are looking at TransExperiafax as a potential profit. TransExperiafax maintains some 500 million personal credit files and another 50 million company credit files. If we say the average company is ten people, that means there are essentially 1 billion personal credit files worth of data that they maintain. If the average credit file on the dark web sells for $5, that means the potential profit of compromising TransExperiafax is $5 billion. So, the attacker is going to evaluate the cost benefit of their malicious cyber pursuits against a potential $5 billion payout.

Using these numbers, maybe a criminal organization has decided they are willing to risk spending 1% of the potential 5-billion-dollar payout over a year, divided quarterly. Figure 3-2 shows what their cyber operations expenditure would look like

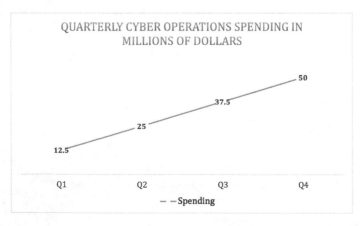

Figure 3-2. *Attacker Cost Benefit*

Summary

The point is that a target organization who is only able to see half of the cost benefit perspective picture is going to do cost benefit analysis on cybersecurity implementations without all the necessary information. If TransExperiafax did this, they would evaluate how much they should spend on cybersecurity using a 1–3.5-billion-dollar benchmark. Would they spend more or make different decisions if they knew that to the attacker, they looked like a $5 billion pay day?

Appropriate cost benefit analysis for cybersecurity products, capabilities, and services needs to at least consider both sides of this analysis and incorporate them into their decision process. Figure 3-3 illustrates the disparity in spending based on perspectives and shows that the attackers would always be spending more than the defenders. A key point too though is that this is just one attacker, maybe there are three, maybe there are many more, maybe they all go after TransExperafax this year, maybe each year, maybe consecutively.

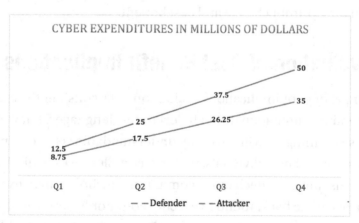

Figure 3-3. Comparing Spending

Understanding Cost Benefit Implications

While understanding the different perspectives of cost benefit is beneficial, it is also necessary to track the implications of implementing a given product, capability, or service. This means that even if on the surface a cybersecurity thing may look cost beneficial, we must also consider how the implementation of that thing alters the rest of our architecture. Primarily this means understanding how risk and work move around an organization as a result of such implementations and if those implications potentially negate the benefits of face value cost benefit analysis.

Risk and Work Are Never Destroyed (ish)

Much like matter, it is hard to destroy risk and effort. OK, with cybersecurity it is not so absolute. However, when cybersecurity things are marketed and sold and consumed, they are often done in a way that is dismissive of risk and work implications and instead focuses heavily, if not entirely, on the up-front change and cost benefit.

Poor Evaluation of Cost Benefit Implications

As an example of poor implications evaluation, let's consider the example of implementing automation through declarative languages. Put very simply, this is coming up with an easily understandable set of commands that, when executed by individuals, perform complex tasks behind the scenes. For instance, the declarative command 'newhost' might execute several scripts in the background to execute commonly performed tasks when a new virtual machine is stood up. It leverages a virtual machine API to create the virtual computer, it adds it to the domain, it creates a user profile on the machine, it installs antivirus and a suite of tools necessary for people to perform their job functions.

The face value of such an implementation is that instead of having a systems engineering team having to manually go through those tasks for each new machine they can simply type 'newhost' using the declarative language interpreter, and all the scripts and execution is orchestrated in the background through automation. This allows for the gaining of efficiencies in setup times for new machines, saves hourly wages paid to admins as they set up hosts and reduces the risk of mistakes by humans during the setup process that could make machines vulnerable. Easy sell right? Unfortunately, these benefits don't take into account where certain risk and work have moved to, and at what point the moves become worth it.

Good Cost Benefit Implications Evaluation

Using the same example, let's walk through what implications should be included in the cost benefit evaluation of a solution like this. There are several impacts to an organization when automation of this nature is put in place. Instead of spending a few hours here and there setting up a new machine for each new hire, an immense amount of work is put in up front to set up the automation mechanisms themselves. There is a clear need to understand what this work looks like and at what put the up-front cost starts to pay off and for how long it pays off. If it cost $100,000 in billable hours to set up the automation, but each machine set up only costs $100 in billable hours, we would have to have a thousand new machines set up before we start to see cost benefit in this regard. That might be easy in a very large organization; in a smaller one, it might not make sense to pursue this type of automation.

There is also the fact that such automation, scripting, and orchestration require specialized skillsets in a system engineering team that were not required before and additional personnel may need to get hired or time spent training them. These issues would add more impact to the cost benefit analysis on implementing this solution. There is also the

51

important movement of risk. Sure, human error is less likely to happen as humans are performing less actions. On the other hand, a single mistake at the orchestration level could not put every subsequent machine create at risk. There is another implication that must be considered in any cost benefit analysis: Where did the risk move to?

A Litmus Test for Cost Benefit

To this point, we have covered detailed methods and examples surrounding the concept of cybersecurity cost benefit, which in truth is simply true cost benefit for an organization. I would like to describe something I use as a quick litmus for cybersecurity things before I even go down the road of a comprehensive cost benefit analysis.

I refer to it as the 1-9-90 principle. The values may vary over time, but the point being made is that essentially, there are three types of threats that make up 1%, 9%, and 90% of cyber actors. Roughly 1% (probably less) of cyber actors are nation-state-level cybersecurity threats, another 9% are APTs and organized crime, and the other 90% are unorganized crime and script kiddies.

The 1% are undeterrable, unpreventable sources using almost completely if not completely unknown capabilities and the best way to deal with such risks are to find ways to accept that they could happen and find ways of living with them such as resilience and redundancy solutions.

The 9% are potentially detectable but unlikely to be preventable as they use both known and unknown capabilities.

The other 90% of cyber threats are those that must be prevented as they involve only known techniques and tools that can be scanned for and or caught by existing security tools.

So how does the litmus work? Well, if someone says they are developing a tool that can prevent nation-state-level APTs or detect them, you should take that claim with a grain of salt. As a purchaser or implementer of such a technology, you risk having sunk cost and resources into something that can't possibly deliver on what it claims. This 1-9-90 principle can be a great guiding resource for R&D as well, as you should focus on developing solutions that are aimed at mitigating specific threat actor sophistications in the most efficient and feasible ways. On the other end of the spectrum would be someone saying we should just accept the risk of the 90%; when you could easily thwart such known capabilities, why would you spend money on being resilient against them? Figure 3-4 illustrates this principle through a simple matrix.

	Tools / Techniques	Type of Actor	Risk Mitigation
1%	Unknown to public	Nation state	Accept
9%	Unknown and known	Organized crime	Detect
90%	Known to public	Unorganized crime	Prevent

Figure 3-4. *1-9-90 Principle*

If we look back at the moving target defense (MTD) example from Chapter 1 and applied this litmus, we probably wouldn't have to bother with further analysis. As the concept claims to PREVENT a 1% capability like a zero day, it would fail out litmus as striving toward an inappropriate method for risk mitigation. Of course, although 1-9-90 could be .001%, 9.999%, and 90% or have some other variance, the point is more that the majority of threats can be prevented; we should try to make sure we detect those that can't be prevented, but we should also acknowledge that there are unpreventable threats that we need to find a way to accept by being resilient to their manifestation. As with any rule or principle, there are surely exceptions; this is simply a quick sniff test ability to provide litmus to the cost benefit analysis of a given cybersecurity paradigm.

Summary

Turns out business thinking or operational thinking is really necessary to understand cybersecurity cost benefit. Additionally, we need to understand the cost benefit of a cybersecurity thing from the perspective of the defender and the attacker in any scenario. We also need to make sure we follow through on in-depth analysis of secondary and tertiary impacts on the resources and risk of an organization after a new cybersecurity thing is implemented. The 1-9-90 principle can enable an efficient, quick litmus to cybersecurity things and their potential cost benefit. Trying to be more secure is not always the right answer, and face value gains in efficiencies or decreases in risk are not always the full story. In later chapters, we will discuss some theoretical cybersecurity concepts that aim to provide real cost benefit. Even though, at the end of the day, our industry, like any other, is about business and not about cybersecurity at all, that doesn't mean the body of work itself can't be. Further, as an industry, if we can do a better job of putting forth feasible cybersecurity things with true cost benefit by leveraging the right kinds of people and context in our theoretical work, cybersecurity vendors, consumers, and professionals will all be the better for it.

CHAPTER 4

Roles and Responsibilities

We are doing a bad job of drawing the line on what is and is not the responsibility of cybersecurity professionals, services, and products. If we continue to fail to understand ourselves and our roles and responsibilities, we cannot hope to innovate on how to improve. Cybersecurity should be defined as the protection of data through transit, processing, and storage, but there has been a large drift away from what true cybersecurity is and how it is employed. Cybersecurity has become all-encompassing in private business, throughout the government, and in our personal lives.

You hear the term everywhere and everything that beeps or squeaks now falls under the umbrella of cybersecurity. With everything now being connected or the Internet of Things (IoT), the area of responsibility now being levied on the cybersecurity professional is becoming unsustainable both fiscally and technologically in providing the protection in the areas truly needed. We must ask ourselves if we are inviting more risk and a larger attack surface all for connivance and appeasement of the employee to stay connected.

Just by looking at the devices that are now permitted if not issued in the workplace, it is easy to see how the cyber footprint has grown tremendously. These added devices, be it laptops, tablets, or smart phones, are often allowed to leave and connect to other networks and then return and reconnect to the company's managed network. This

© Dr. Jacob G. Oakley, Michael Butler, Wayne York, Dr. Matthew Puckett, Dr. J. Louis Sewell 2022
J. G. Oakley et al., *Theoretical Cybersecurity*, https://doi.org/10.1007/978-1-4842-8300-4_4

simple and now wildly accepted practice is the responsibility of your cybersecurity professional to manage and defend. Even if these devices are company-owned and managed, it is added time, expense, and human capital to manage and protect these devices. This same problem exists with the bring your own device (BYoD) to work programs if it doesn't bring more risks to the company. It must be asked why it is now so widely accepted to introduce so much risk to a network for the possible increase in productivity from those who use these devices.

If productivity is the driving factor for BYoD and the issuing of digital devices to employees, then it must be weighed against the cost it will incur for supporting those decisions. The cybersecurity team will now have to draft a policy for end users' agreement, identify tools and techniques for scanning reporting. The team will now have to expend more man-hours to secure and defend all the extra devices in the name of productivity. There may be added cost of new software and licensing depending on existing licensing and tools used by the team. How is productivity measured for using these devices? Is it the number of emails received and responded to? Or is it by word count on documents created while not connected to the company's network?

Responsibilities to Shed

It is important to note that the medium through which a security or disingenuous act is precipitated through is not necessarily the reason it happens. As an example, think back to the by-mail scams of the 1990s wherein alleged royalty of other nations promised wealth in return for a tiny bit of help. This has become a notorious and meme-worthy scam where the victim offers a check or cash or money order to help this royal get out of their country or somehow otherwise obtain their new inheritance or wealth. Plenty of people fell for this scam and sent money or wasted time and effort trying to get the bigger pay day on the other end of the scam, which never came.

Now, this scam was facilitated through the US Postal Service (USPS). The inherent trust in something delivered to your mailbox by a uniformed governmental official lent credence to the contents of the scam letters and was undoubtedly part of what enabled them. However, no one would argue that this was a form of mail-attack or a mail-security issue. Why is it that when someone accomplishes the exact same scam through email that we call it a cyberattack or cybersecurity issue? The USPS certainly didn't offer up any responsibility for what you or the scammer did across its communications medium (the mail).

This is a bit of an oversimplification, but it paints the picture clearly on why there are certainly malicious activities taking place through the cyber domain that cybersecurity professionals are at best, overextending themselves by being on the hook for mitigating. At worst, this gives the perception that cybersecurity is not working in instances where it has not even been allowed input to a situation. Without shedding such examples, cybersecurity innovation and theory will be hard to foster due to overextension and widespread misconception about what cybersecurity should be and should focus on. The following are both real and fictitious case studies that illustrate several other areas where cybersecurity should shed its responsibility and rebuff attempts to include such activities in its purview. This is not exhaustive, and there are certainly more; the point to be taken is that an examination of what is and is not a cybersecurity issue must happen for theoretical cybersecurity to thrive.

Case Study 1

Mirroring similar real-world examples of fraud, in this case study, our victims had millions of dollars in crypto currency stolen from their account by ultimately putting themselves in a position to reset a crypto-wallet user's password and logging in to their account and transferring out funds.

What Happened

The thief (I am not saying hacker) took publicly available emails of senior executives of a crypto-wallet company that were published to that company's websites and used them as logins. The phone numbers of those individuals were found through simply looking them up on professional networking websites. The thief then went to the crypto-wallet user site, where at least one of these senior executives surely had an account (they admitted to using their own wallet service on both their website and professional networking profiles to lend credibility to it).

On the crypto-wallet site, the thief entered into one of the email accounts that bore the username and hit password reset. But before they did this, they had done an illegal SIM swap on their cellphone to register it with the phone number of the executive's cellphone. Before the cell network deconflicted this error, the thief was able to receive the password reset text for the crypto-wallet application and input their own new password. Then the thief simply logged in and sent the funds to their own account.

Why It Is Inappropriate

This is more akin to traditional identity theft and fraud, and no code-execution, hack, or vulnerability was exploited from a cybersecurity perspective. Similar stories to this fictitious case study have been published on prominent cybersecurity forums and websites and across those and more traditional media are discussed as hacks and cybersecurity vulnerabilities, which only further permeates such misunderstanding.

Who Is Responsible

Theft like this is the responsibility of the victim, for publishing information that is used as their username, as well as data on what devices would be used to accomplish resetting the password. Perhaps, this could be considered an issue with the cell network allowing SIM swapping to redirect traffic from one phone to the other. In neither case though, is this a cybersecurity issue.

Case Study 2

Crypto currency has exploded onto the scene in the past decade and for a while, new coins were being announced frequently and with no official, legal, or defensible verification process. What followed were events called initial coin offerings (ICOs) which pulled credibility from the similar initial public offering (IPO) for companies wishing to go public and generate funding. Essentially, the ICO was a company saying, if we get a certain amount of people to invest money into our crypto currency, we can launch it and be another successful, but probably smaller, version of Bitcoin, Ethereum, or others. This can also be done as a scam for malicious reasons too and result in ordinary theft.

What Happened

In this case study though, the thieves were pretending to stand up a new crypto currency and published and advertised their new ICO on a website they bought and paid for to appear as legitimate as possible. The scammers even registered a company with the same name and had a connivingly professional URL and technical jargon to convince would-be investors of the strength of the security in their crypto currency. With this scam infrastructure in place, they started their ICO event.

Once the ICO event concluded though, investors did not receive their crypto currency or accounts in crypto wallets listing their new digital assets. The thieves had simply gone through the effort of pretending to host an ICO and all of the investors had simply sent money to them and would receive nothing in turn. There is a twist though. The website the scammers registered put up a lone post, saying that during their ICO they had been the victims of a hack and that they were terribly sorry for anyone's losses or inconveniences, but since they had also put all of their funds into the ICO as well, they were being forced to file for bankruptcy and liquidate the business.

In truth though, the scammers had not been hacked, they just used it as an excuse because it had happened to several other early ICOs. They said the attackers moved all the funds into some other account. But in this case, there was no actual hack or attack and the scammers had simply transferred the funds to another account themselves, using the fictitious hack as cover.

Why It Is Inappropriate

Once again, here there is no code vulnerability leveraged or exploitation that has happened. There is no hack that led to the compromise of the website and the victims have simply been duped into sending money just as in Case Study 1. There is nothing a cybersecurity professional should do here. While, in Case Study 1, it was media attention and cybersecurity forums that intonated it was a cybersecurity issue at hand, in this case study, it was the scammers themselves that sought to leverage the overextension of cybersecurity's boundaries for their own good.

Who Is Responsible

The obvious answer is the scammers are responsible for this since it was them who stole the money. But the individuals who bought into this scam bear some responsibility as well. These scammers knew they could prey on the eagerness of inexperienced investors to not do their due diligence and try and get rich quick. The difference in how this impacts the establishment of boundaries for cybersecurity compared to Case Study 1 is important. In the first example, the victims of email scams and the media are typically the ones crying foul against cybersecurity for not having prevented the email solicitation scam. In this case study, it was the thieves that pushed the blame on to cybersecurity. Both are an impediment to the craft of cybersecurity, putting the body of work in an unflattering light via overextension of responsibility boundaries.

Case Study 3

In a militarily invaded country, a satellite Internet provider for the sake of altruism seeks to provide free Internet to the recently deprived citizens of that country, so they can continue to communicate despite the aggressor's attempts to destroy the IT infrastructure of the country. Unfortunately, electronic warfare (EW) emissions were being used by the aggressor to negate the capabilities of this newly delivered satellite Internet as well.

What Happened

The satellite Internet vendor publicly denounces the invader's attempt to jam and negate the vendor's ability to provide this vital service of Internet access to the citizens of the attacked country. In social media, the vendor's CEO even states that they have taken cybersecurity and other efforts necessary to protect their system from the effects of the enemy's EW jamming.

Why It Is Inappropriate

In truth, the fix to the issue was that a software update to the software-defined radio (SDR) components of the Internet service systems was able to get around the invader jamming certain frequencies by simply adjusting to new frequencies as was necessary. Neither the issue (jamming) nor the solution (updating programming) is a cybersecurity issue or solution. The implementation was done on digital devices (SDRs are essentially computers attached to antenna), but this is far outside the realm of cybersecurity.

Who Is Responsible

As stated, this was a programmed update to address the EW problem. Foresight on the part of the vendor could have enabled them to create programs that were capable of addressing degraded environments on their own. Even so, it was the vendor's electronic radio frequency specialists and programmers that fixed the issue, not cybersecurity professionals or solutions. So, why mention this case study at all? We have brought it up because while the first two case studies had the victim and then the thief being responsible for inappropriately roping in cybersecurity into the conversation, here we have a vendor themselves doing so. More careful messaging on social media as to the issue at hand and the fix and leaving out the term cybersecurity from that particular message would have prevented any potential interpretation of cybersecurity responsibility in this instance.

Responsibilities to Embrace

It is one thing to shirk responsibilities for cybersecurity where appropriate and sometimes necessary. As we have discussed, this is for the betterment of the industry as well as our consumers. It would be lazy to think that there are then no situations where cybersecurity as an industry or body of work could step in and provide further or previously unacknowledged benefit. These situations are likely to be more niche in nature and harder to come by, and admittedly, the issue at hand for this chapter is focused on the hampering nature of overextension. Still, if we are doing an introspective analysis, we should evaluate both sides of the argument.

Example: Be Your Own Enemy

The best example of something we believe could be considered a novel and beneficial approach to applying traditional cybersecurity roles and mentalities is an offensive assessment. In this book and others, the concept of offensive security are covered as truly proactive ways of securing an organization's attack surface by applying traditional (military) red team mentality to cybersecurity assessment in the form of services like penetration testing.

Our argument is that that mindset should be applied to other aspects of the risk equation. A penetration tester might look at an organization's computer or network and try to find ways of exploiting it or using it to exploit the organization. We argue for taking the mindset and applying it to things like cost-benefit and intelligence creation as well. Leveraging the attacker or red team mindset and assessing an organization provides insight into how cyber criminals might view that organization as a target. This can reveal the ways in which those adversaries may consider their own unique cost benefits when trying to compromise the organization. Further, this mindset could be applied to create cyber threat intelligence that could be used by the organization to help it secure itself through informing of hunt and detect activities. This sort of implementation allows an organization to focus not only on threat intelligence from known cyber threats and actors but to postulate their own, with their complete insider knowledge in ways that may prove uniquely insightful and help mitigate cyber risk in unconventional ways.

Learning to Leverage the Non-Cyber

There are non-cyber decisions that can be made by those not in cybersecurity that can impact the posture and attack surface of an organization more effectively that cybersecurity solutions. If it is important to know what things to acknowledge cybersecurity should not be responsible for or things that should potentially be added, it is also important to know when cybersecurity is better served through un-security efforts.

What if there was a way to combine two things in one place without jeopardizing that which is most important? If the new normal is that everyone is going to be allowed to have access to all their personal accounts at work, then how do organizations and their cybersecurity professionals make sure their policies are implemented and enforced to protect their data while allowing employees their ability to use personal accounts? what if there was a way to allow this without the accounts of the employees having to ever touch the organization's network or having access to the organization's data?

Could a simple separation of two networks be the solution? The organization could have their network that would be restricted to only the applications and data that are truly needed for the employees to perform their jobs and the mission of the organization. Another network could be stood up and accessible to all employees but would be open and more of a use-at-your-own-risk, with minimal resources being spent monitoring or defending it. The restricted network would be the cybersecurity professional's sole responsibility to defend and operate as it will contain all the organization's data. While the open network will allow for employees to use for personal applications such as social media and checking personal email accounts, it will not contain any data from the organization. While there is an added cost for providing the open network with separate hardware and another service contract with an Internet provider, there is a reduction in risk and less man-hours spent trying to monitor and defend the organization's network from every employee's personal accounts. This would be a low-cost solution that reduces risk to the organization while providing Internet access for employees to use for personal applications.

Example 1

Assume you are the CISO of a company that makes sneakers. You are reviewing your organization's cybersecurity resources, such as staff and software licensing, because there is a cut to funding and the ask from the organization has been to find something to cut. Log and traffic monitoring is one of the highest cost expenditures your organization has from both a staffing and a licensing standpoint. The licensing for the software used to collect, aggregate, and analyze logged events and network traffic flow within the organization charges on a traffic-volume basis. Further, because of the amount of traffic being collected, analysis and response to incidents by cybersecurity staff make up a bulk of the hours allotted from a salary standpoint in the cybersecurity department.

After a quick look through these resources, you find it difficult to cut other cybersecurity personnel or software requirements, so you return to the log and traffic collection issue. You notice that almost 25% of the traffic collected, aggregated, and analyzed for malicious activity are entirely from social media websites and platforms that are in no way involved in the operation of the organization or the execution of tasks toward accomplishing strategic goals. If this sort of network traffic was simply denied, from both a policy and filtering standpoint, there would be an extra 10% personnel hours and software budget overall for the cybersecurity department which would meet the necessity of the proposed budget cuts and would not detract from the security posture of the organization or the defense of its cyberattack surface.

This means you can reduce the budget, which aids the organization in accomplishing its strategic goals. Further, the organization's risk exposure is also lowered as common mediums for various attacks and exfiltration of sensitive information have been removed from the network. This was accomplished without any need for further cybersecurity implementations or solutions and should be an example of a first step that could be taken by an organization to address its cyber risk and not a last-ditch defensive effort by the cybersecurity department to avoid budget cuts. It is again an oversimplification of a situation within an organization, but it illustrates the importance of understanding where the boundaries of cybersecurity roles and responsibilities lie and how non-cybersecurity efforts can make them easier to maintain.

Example 2

Let's continue with the same role and company as Example 1. You are the CISO and the business model is to sell sneakers, as many as possible for as long as possible. That would be the business strategy of the organization. The CEO has tasked you with using some of your cybersecurity budget to ensure the organization can withstand the impacts of cyber compromise and continue operations.

You begin researching implementations for servers and user machines to be more resilient to individual cyber compromises so that they don't end up having larger, more widespread impacts on the business. You find that such virtualized solutions come with their own cost models, and they are in some places cheaper, and in others, much more expensive than your current architecture. In all cases, however, because you do not currently operate in the cloud or a virtualized environment, they are a new cost. Further, going with said solutions can result in a sort of waste of already sunk costs in physical infrastructure you already operate from as they would fall into obsolescence.

Worse still, you do not have in-house cybersecurity expertise to correctly leverage these technologies and platforms, which means even more money would have to be spent on training or hiring. You know the CEO's goal is resilience to cyber compromise and to avoid that as a risk to the business strategy. What if you challenged the rest of the organization to help mitigate such risks from non-cyber perspectives? What sets your sneaker company apart from others is that you allow custom orders of sneakers, and they are then processed and made to order and sent out.

The same chain of devices that handles orders also carries credit card information from the purchaser to the company's accounting department. This means that risk to company operations and risk to customer data ride along the same paths and that compromise of any device along this chain of devices can impact both revenue and reputation.

You ask if it would be possible to have the order placed on the website send that data directly to the shoe manufacturing devices and those devices would then send an appropriate invoice to the accounting department. This would allow the accounting devices to then send an invoice to the purchaser, ensuring that financial data only passed from customer to accounting and that shoe creation data only passed from customer to manufacturing devices. This separates the revenue and potential reputation risks into segmented parts of the organization and would make both sides more resilient to a ransomware attack in one or the other. This allows for non-cyber decision makers to weigh in on a situation that can simplify the architecture the cybersecurity staff have to protect without turning it into a tax on the organization's operations.

This sort of example can also exist in a completely non-cyber state where doing something as simple as spending the money to create a three-month stockpile of certain ingredients for sneakers would make you resilient to threats such as ransomware on your logistics and ordering servers. If the three-month supply of sneaker ingredients and storage of them is cheaper than the cybersecurity solution to make the logistics servers resilient, it would probably be better to go with the non-cyber option. This is especially the case because an on-hand supply increase like that is something that will always eventually be utilized and will be seen by someone such as a CEO as less of a dead cost or paid tax than cybersecurity might.

Building the Right Size Box

Typically, we security professionals are preaching outside the box thinking, but perhaps, as illustrated by previous examples that has maybe gotten us overextended. The motivation may have been to broaden consumer's exposure to cybersecurity, but that lens is probably too wide. These decisions should be tailored and right sized to fit the organization's strategic goals and be appropriate to the resources available to that organization or otherwise inform the accumulation of those necessary resources.

Everything is now connected, and everyone has multiple devices that they carry with them everywhere they go. There are smart watches, smart phones, and even smart glasses; everything is becoming smart and, in doing so, allowing constant access to the Internet. It's this constant connection that must be evaluated to determine what risks we are willing to accept and why.

To understand where to draw the line or what is to be allowed in the cybersecurity box, there must be a true understanding of what devices are critical from a cyber perspective for a company to complete its intended purpose. This one piece of knowledge can help to stop the mission creep for cybersecurity professionals inside the company. When trying to apply cybersecurity without the internal knowledge of what truly needs to be protected, the security can become thin and/or overstretched trying to protect everything. Focusing on protecting from the inside out allows you to identify where areas can be included rather than a blanket security policy. The one size fits all for cybersecurity practice is both human and computer resource-ineffective.

Allocating cyber resources to critical areas and reducing or eliminating them in areas that are not directly related to productivity or are simply a nicety for the employee allows for a more focused implementation of resources. With this information, you now know the bare minimum that must be supported and protected. This may, when really looked at, be a server in a closet with only a few truly needed connections to it.

There needs to be a self-assessment of what a likely attack on your organization would actually be and what would be the targeted area inside the network. In the news, there are countless reports of ransomware being deployed against local governments, the natural gas industry, and other organizations. These organizations all provide products or services that, if they were unavailable, would cause a considerable disruption. There is also a presumption that, if ransomware was deployed, there is an ability to pay the requested ransom. What does your organization provide? Should there be reason for concern of a ransomware attack? Would the value of your data be more valuable than the service you provide? Then there is the fear of data exfiltration that must be considered.

Understanding what your organizations value as a target will focus resources and help identify potential attack types. As a small company, the likelihood of being targeted with ransomware is probably lower since there is less perceived money for the attacker to receive. Conversely, if your organization has data of high value of individuals or other organizations, then that information may be seen as more valuable and therefore a targeted resource. There is always the chance of random attacks against the organization. So, what does building an appropriately sized box for a specific organization's cybersecurity look like?

Step 1: Know Thy Cyber-Self

In Chapter 2, we discussed how the taxonomy of where roles and responsibilities fall within the expansive and diverse body of work that is cybersecurity. To protect any organization with cybersecurity services or products, that organization must clearly understand what the roles and responsibilities are of what resources it already has in place. This requires a more in-depth understanding of the taxonomy of cyber roles that is typically expected or presumed. Without this knowledge though, an appropriate definition of what is and is not the responsibility of those people, services, and products cannot be accomplished.

Step 2: Prevent What Is Known

Before you do anything else or can hope to achieve strategic or theoretical gains in cybersecurity application, the known threats must be prevented first or there is no cost benefit in expanded approaches. The aim of this book is to suggest that the envelope must be expanded or pushed in new directions. However, it would be folly to not accept that there are minimum, non-theoretical efforts that must be in place before innovation and improvement can be pursued. Known threats and existing vulnerabilities are things that must be focused on first and foremost. To spend time on theoretical or novel cybersecurity applications in the hopes of better addressing risk within the constraints of cost benefit before doing so is foolhardy.

If available cybersecurity resources cannot prevent or mitigate what is known and already observed as cyber threats and risks, there is no sense leveraging them in other ways. This statement is not meant to stymie efforts at improving the body of work that is cybersecurity. It is to ensure that innovation takes place responsibly, after what should be commonly implemented countermeasures and protections are already in place. To do otherwise risks unsophisticated compromise that endangers cybersecurity consumers and the reputation of cybersecurity producers.

Step 3: Know Thy Strategic Self

Beyond knowing what cybersecurity assets are at the disposal of an organization, it is also imperative that the organization and its cybersecurity staff understand the long-term goals and tasks (cyber and non-cyber) that are integral to the organization. Without this knowledge, it is impossible to establish cost benefit in general or as it specifically relates to resource expenditure on cybersecurity to protect said goals and tasks from risks to its attack surface. Without knowledge of cost benefit and risks in this sense, the cyber box may have boundary lines based on available abilities, but what they are placed around is yet unknown.

Step 4: Leverage Non-Cyber

As was shown in several examples earlier in this chapter, risks to an organization are not always best addressed through cybersecurity implementations. Further, cybersecurity issues and risks can at times be more efficiently mitigated through non-cybersecurity choices and implementations. The potential for these sorts of solutions should be assessed and exhausted before cybersecurity is fully leaned on to solve various problems. This means that security staff need to be empowered to prevent the baseline, known, preventable threats and then be brought into conversations regarding an organization's strategic tasks and goals, so they can participate in the enabling of said goals and tasks and whether cybersecurity is the best or most cost-beneficial solution available.

Most consumers of cybersecurity are not cybersecurity producers. It should therefore go without saying that leaning on an organization's organic and native expertise to address risks first, cyber or otherwise, will lead to the most efficient solutions to such problems.

Step 5: Calibrate and Implement

At this point, we have identified our organization's cybersecurity resources and their roles and responsibilities. We have enabled them to prevent the bare-minimum acceptable number of cyber risks based on known threats. We have informed the cybersecurity apparatus on what the strategic goals and risks of the organization are, and the organization has worked together with its cybersecurity staff to burn down additional risks with non-cyber solutions where able and appropriate. Next, we should look to adjust roles and responsibilities that are carried out on our cybersecurity resources to focus on what is most necessary to achieve good cost benefit, while only expecting cybersecurity personnel, services, and products to function within established boundaries of responsibility. At this point, it may be necessary to expand or contract in certain functional areas of the cybersecurity taxonomy to achieve the most cost-beneficial results necessary, only after exhausting internal non-cyber solutions as well. Aside from leveraging tribal knowledge and organizational expertise, such solutions have the benefit of being viewed as less of a sunk cost or tax, as the operational staff of the organization more readily understand the cost benefit of such implementations that reduce risk. Whereas, in cyber this may be harder to communicate.

Step 6: Reassessment

It is not enough to identify and calibrate an organization's cybersecurity response to strategic risks once. Any successful enterprise, commercial or otherwise, relies on adaptability to environments and events as well as the passage of time to stay relevant and operational and maintain strategic continuity. Any periodic re-evaluation that supports these goals and tasks must also include cyclical recalibration of the cybersecurity apparatus that supports the risk mitigation of that organization. Figure 4-1 illustrates this process.

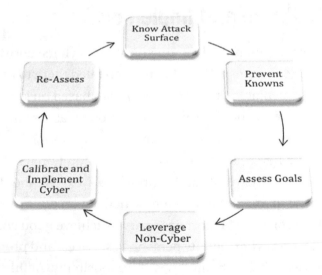

Figure 4-1. *Building the right sized cybersecurity box*

Summary

We have discussed in this chapter that one of the bigger challenges to successful cybersecurity and cybersecurity innovation and theorization is poorly defined boundaries. Our ability to define what roles and responsibilities fall within and on the periphery of our body of work is integral to having a strong foundation from which innovation can build upon. The case studies presented, and the process proposed are just our examples on ways to understand how organizationally specific boundaries can be established. This will allow us to address cybersecurity risk appropriately with resources that are not overextended. We will learn how to communicate with the wider organization in ways that present cybersecurity risks as addressable through non-cyber means. Further, through cyclical establishment, analysis, and defense of appropriate roles and responsibilities we can better position theoretical cybersecurity innovation on both a by-organization and body of work basis.

CHAPTER 5

Experimentation

Technology-specific solutions traditionally lend themselves to straightforward assessments of success via measurable results. The ability to determine whether or not a new technology provides a better metric as a solution to a problem is a foundational portion of any argument for its acceptance. The following analysis of established security paradigms and their respective evaluation via experimental methods will highlight the need for a differing process to provide defensible measurement of success or failure of human reliant cybersecurity implementation evaluations, which, given that attackers are humans, is all of them.

Unlike technologies, cybersecurity implementation assessment does not easily provide statistical metrics indicative of effectiveness. The art and tradecraft involved in such assessments mean that the same individuals could assess the same type of network and implementation multiple times and have different paths, discoveries, and recommendations. Additionally, the statistics that could be measured do not necessarily reflect the quality of work. If one type of assessment found 100 vulnerabilities and another type found 10, it might be deduced that the one which found 100 was the better assessment method. Part of what makes cybersecurity assessment methodologies difficult to compare is that it could be that the 10 vulnerabilities found in one assessment were of higher impact and importance than the 100 found in the other.

Not only is the cybersecurity implementation assessment process heavily reliant on human involvement from an attacker standpoint but the validation of its results requires implementations by yet another group of

J. G. Oakley et al., *Theoretical Cybersecurity*, https://doi.org/10.1007/978-1-4842-8300-4_5

humans performing systems administration, configuration, and operation.
Then the organizational security must be reevaluated by a third group
of humans to establish if there was change in the security posture. Here
there is an issue where typical analysis of quantitative data is not only
insufficient but likely unavailable in the way other security technologies
might measure performance. Success of any given concept can be shown
with defensible evaluation of the human tradecraft-driven assessment.
To accomplish this, a framework for evaluating one cybersecurity
implementation against another is necessary to allow for measuring their
individual success and comparable novelty.

Identifying Requirements for Defensible Evaluation

Before designing an experiment to verify the novelty and quality of a
cybersecurity implementation, experiment defensibility requirements
need to be established. The following requirements toward defensibility
should be met to standardize the actions of the human actors in the
evaluation of cybersecurity paradigms:

- Controlled and realistic environment

- Defensible configuration

- Defensible operation

- Defensible Emulation

- Measurable results and metrics

Controlled and Realistic Environment

Since the goal of an experiment regarding a cybersecurity implementation
is to identify how well it provides mitigation for threats and risks, it must be

conducted in an environment that represents exemplar real-world targets where such an implementation would be deployed. If assessments were done against unrealistic target networks, there would be no translation to success or failure of the paradigm in actual implementations. Control is important with regard to both users and administrators of a given network as well as outside actors attempting to compromise it. For example, if offensive cybersecurity assessors conducting one type of assessment, for instance, were able to leverage a communications path opened by the user running a Virtual Private Network (VPN), the assessment might have findings from a separate part of the organization. If assessors running another type of assessment against the same organization encountered no users running the VPN software during the time window for the assessment, they would never have a chance to generate the same findings and recommendations. This type of unfairness in an uncontrolled environment can be shown by any number of other examples such as outages in one location or another. For instance, a certain machine could be powered off during one assessment and during another, the machines might all be powered on. It is therefore clear that any evaluation of different offensive security assessments must be conducted in realistic, controlled, and identical environments.

Defensible Configuration

To determine the impact on the security posture of the test systems, configuration and administration must be performed in a repeatable and defensible way. This must also be carried out as realistically as possible. There could be a scenario where the administrator took over 100 hours to implement the changes for one cybersecurity implementation. If the implementation being compared took the administrator ten hours to complete, the comparison between the successes of either version of changes on the network might not be equal.

There is also a possibility that the configurations for one cybersecurity implementation to be evaluated are outside the realm of realistic expectations for systems administration in a real network. If the systems administration were performed improperly or unrealistically, it could provide no added security or potentially make a network more vulnerable, and therefore prevent comparison of the network's security posture. Any experiment aiming to determine the success of different cybersecurity implementations must ensure that systems administration and configuration is performed in an equal, appropriate, and realistic manner between compared paradigms.

Changes implemented by systems administration must also be accurate representations of the intent of the cybersecurity implementations. If the systems administrator misinterpreted what proper configurations were, it would also skew any ability to defensibly compare the success of one type of offensive security assessment over the other.

Defensible Operation

When comparing the effectiveness of two different cybersecurity implementations, the performance of those operating the implementations must be as defensible as possible. Imagine a scenario where one type of offensive cybersecurity assessment is conducted by someone with almost no experience in vulnerability assessment and computer exploitation and the other assessor has over ten years of such experience. The less experienced assessor is not likely to have as many or as impactful findings and is less likely to provide quality recommendations to mitigate those findings. That would be a poor basis to judge the quality of an assessment method against. Any experiment intent on evaluation of cybersecurity implementations must therefore ensure that the operators of that implementation are performed by equally qualified individuals if applicable. This is potentially not the case in a substantial portion of cybersecurity implementations where human operation is not required post configuration. However, in the instances where human operators are involved, they need to be leveraged in a fair and defensible manner.

This is the case for both defensive and offensively oriented cybersecurity implementations. In offensive cybersecurity, the recommendations of the security assessors must be within the bounds of reason for an actual offensive security assessment. An assessor or defender could posit the recommendation of unplugging the organization network from the Internet or blocking all ports on device firewalls, which would certainly mitigate risk of remote exploitation. However, such recommendations are not likely to be applicable to any real-world scenario as they would hinder the operations of the host organization, and therefore would not be part of a real security solution.

Defensible Emulation of a Motivated and Sophisticated Attacker

With regard to evaluating the mitigating factors introduced to systems by cybersecurity implementations, the need for an appropriately emulated, motivated, and sophisticated actor is extremely important. Implementing security changes and then waiting to see if non-emulated attackers are able to compromise different portions of an organization is not defensible. It would be nearly impossible to guarantee a situation where a real cyber-attack was conducted with motivation against host organizations secured by the assessor recommendations. It would also be nearly impossible to determine the true motivation of real actors. The actor going after one network may be only a curious hacker or even an automated attack script and the attack against a second network could be an APT intent on some data or user within the network. Use of non-emulated actors creates an untenable situation for an experiment to present reliable or realistically defensible results.

Defensible emulation of the malicious actor allows the experiment to provide an equally motivated attack campaign against networks secured by cybersecurity implementations and then, as equally and defensibly as possible, determine the ability of those changes to thwart the attacker. There is a necessity to evaluate cybersecured networks to face equal levels of sophistication during the malicious attack campaigns waged against them. Equal motivation and sophistication of threats faced during experimentation is only available via emulated threat actors. This emulated actor should also represent a realistic threat commensurate with what real-world organizations may face. Regardless of actor motivation, if the capabilities for computer exploitation do not extend beyond the use of automated exploit frameworks, the experiment may result in a false sense of security where the network actually possesses little to no defense against real world threats.

Measurable Results and Metrics

If all other requirements for defensible experimental evaluation of cybersecurity implementations can be accomplished, there is still the need to provide a measurable metric. Such a metric must determine the level of success or failure that assessor-recommended changes had in enhancing the security posture and threat mitigation of an organization. Without such a metric, there is no way to determine a quantitative difference between offensive security concepts.

Without measuring the comparative effectiveness of offensive security assessments there is no way to validate a new paradigm as being an improvement upon existing methods in a given situation. As discussed earlier, such a metric must go beyond the number of findings by assessors. For the same reasons, success or failure cannot be measured by the amount of machines compromised by the emulated actor. If the emulated actor compromised ten unimportant user machines in one network, yet in the other compromised two servers, the email server and the file store server, the two would seem to be more dangerous to the organization than the ten. To determine validity of a cybersecurity concept in comparison to others, measurable metrics representing realistic impact to the organization must be identified.

Evaluation Mediums

Potential underlying test beds for cybersecurity experimentation have four possible categorical mediums. The basic traits of these potential experiment mediums are based on the real or simulated nature of the environment and the real or simulated nature of the malicious actors. A real environment is considered for the purpose of this categorization to also have real systems administrators and operators (if necessary) and a simulated environment is considered to have its own simulated systems administration.

Real Network and Operators with Real Attackers

If this scenario were used for an evaluation medium, it would suffer from many drawbacks with regard to satisfying the defensibility requirements this dissertation has levied. With a real network and real attackers, the environment will be realistic and translate to real-world situations. However, there would be no experimental control over the organization or its network. Security assessment would not be defensible as too many environmental variables could differ across the different engagements. Using real systems administrators means that different administrators could perform different changes for the different actors and they may not want to comply with assessor recommendations if they do not agree with them. This would not allow for evaluation of the recommended changes. Relying on real attackers to engage the organization during experimental windows means there is no guarantee on similar attacks, as the sheer breadth of variance in entities targeting organizations can be in the tens of thousands. It can be difficult to determine if a motivated attacker is trying to compromise the host organization during the evaluation period. Further, it would prove almost impossible to determine the level of sophistication of attackers between different evaluation windows, if attackers were present at all. Any metrics gathered during an experiment on such a medium would be unreliable at best and unsatisfactory as experimental results toward the validation of offensive security assessment methods.

Real Network and Operators with Simulated Attackers

If this scenario were used for an evaluation medium, it would also suffer from drawbacks with regard to satisfying the defensibility requirements this dissertation has levied against experimental validation. It is worth noting, however, that the supplement of simulated attackers for real ones does increase the potential for this option.

With a real network and simulated attackers, the environment will be realistic and translate to real-world situations. Like before, there would be no experimental control over the organization or its network. Security assessment would not be defensible as too many environmental variables still exist that may differ across the engagements of the different offensive security assessment methods being evaluated. Using real systems administrators still provides the possibility different administrators could perform different changes for the different assessors and they may not want to comply with assessor recommendations if they do not agree with them. Using simulated attackers allows for an equal level of motivation and sophistication with regard to attacks against the secured networks; however, the presence of real users and real security measures used by the organization still presents pitfalls for successful attack simulation and evaluation. Any metrics gathered during an experiment on such a medium would still be unreliable as too many variables are left uncontrolled and potentially unequal between engagements.

Lab Network with Real Attackers

If this scenario were used for an evaluation medium, it would suffer from limited drawbacks with regard to satisfying the defensibility requirements in the attempt at validation of offensive security assessment paradigms. Use of real attackers on a controlled lab network does increase the defensibility of experimentation; however, it still has issues. A lab network in lieu of a real organization network, using real attackers, would in the immediate seem to present satisfaction for a controlled and realistic environment; this is not fully the case. Multiple real attackers could be acting against the organization at the same time and create the potential for hampering each other's progress as well as possibly creating situations that would allow for unnaturally expedited compromise of systems. There are also liability concerns in such experiments where attackers could leverage the lab network for exploitation of other targets. The lab network can be created in the image of a real organization and therefore translate to real-world situations. Yet, the inability to guarantee behavior of the actor means there is no ability to guarantee control of the lab network throughout the experiment. As long as security assessment of the lab network was conducted prior to being connected to the Internet to face real attackers, the assessment of the network will at least be defensible as environmental variables can be guaranteed to be equal during the assessment periods. As was the case previously with use of real attackers, motivation and sophistication cannot be guaranteed to be defensibly equal across the different engagements of the experiment. In such a setting, it can be difficult to distinguish between what was malicious activity or simply user mistakes. Since there is no guarantee on the effort of the attacker across given engagements, the metrics do not defensibly represent the effect of different assessor recommended changes on the security of networks.

Lab Network with Simulated Attacker

In a scenario conducted on this medium, an experiment is capable of achieving all of the defensibility requirements levied by this dissertation. Utilization of a lab network allows for a controlled environment. So long as it is created in the image of a real organization, it will be realistic, and findings of experiments conducted on it will translate to real-world scenarios. Security assessments conducted against controlled environments are defensible as the environmental variables can be maintained across assessment engagements. Systems administration conducted by experiment actors on the environment allows for defensible and equal representation of security change implementation. The motivation and sophistication of the simulated attacker can be guaranteed to be equal across the different campaigns and therefore defensible. Given the control over the realistic network and simulation of realistic actors during the experiment, this medium can provide measurable metrics that provide useable results for the validation of offensive security assessment paradigms.

Evaluation Mediums Summary

Clearly, there are pros and cons to picking a various-evaluation medium for the cybersecurity implementation evaluation to be conducted across. The most important thing is to understand the issues each of them face and to pick the most appropriate medium in a defensible manner. Doing this ensures that the evaluation medium has as little impact on the successful evaluation experiment as possible. Further, knowing the drawbacks and advantages of the chosen medium allows for experiment design to reflect further attempts at defensibility.

Experimentation Example

As an example, the following is a walkthrough of the experiment design and defensibility considerations I implemented for my doctoral dissertation, where I was evaluating the novel offensive cybersecurity assessment paradigm of *Counter-APT Red Teaming*. For more information on the concept itself, my *Professional Red Teaming* book, also by Apress, or my dissertation published by ProQuest contains exhaustive details. Here I am simply using it to illustrate what a best effort at defensibility in cybersecurity implementation evaluation looks like.

Experiment Design

With the goals of this experiment being to compare a new process for offensive cybersecurity assessment against more traditional red teaming, I determined that it requires a realistic lab network with cybersecurity implementations operated by real people, if necessary, and emulated threats and experiment actors. This is the medium I feel is best used to contrast two processes in a specific scenario.

With an evaluation medium determined for the experiment to be built upon, it is important to pick a target for the offensive security assessment that allows the experiment to provide results that would translate to a real scenario. For this purpose, there is a further requirement for identifying a simulated target that would provide an opportunity to represent the type of environment that would provide identifiable priority items for the CAPTR team model.

Target Determination to Support Realistic Network

The example of a law firm was chosen to be the basis for the lab network. A law firm contains data such as attorney–client privileged information as well as information being used in on-going legal cases. If compromised, such objects would likely be so damaging to the organization it would cease to operate. This example also allows for separate segments of a network containing operational personnel in one area and legal personnel in another. Unlike other probable targets of motivated advanced malicious actors, the legal firm example allows for a relatively small network of 40 to 50 machines to be used. This is in comparison to those of a large corporation or government institutions that would also likely be the target of such attacks. In a simulated law firm, there is no need to emulate specialized equipment such as medical or SCADA devices, which could prove difficult for experiment designers. The presence of such technology would also levy a need for specialized skills in security assessment, systems administration, and simulated attacker, which would make finding experiment actors a challenge.

Experiment Summary

CAPTR team methodology experimentation must defensibly answer two questions. Does CAPTR teaming identify findings that are unique to those found using offensive security assessors following more traditional processes? Do the recommendations from such assessments stand up in the face of advanced adversaries? Answering these questions allows for a measured representation of the uniqueness of findings generated via the CAPTR team paradigm and the ability of such findings to mitigate risk in the face of advanced motivated actors such as APTs.

With the goal of answering both questions, three identical copies of a network were created. The networks were built with only functionality in mind and were created to represent a small law firm of forty-two machines.

In this network, there were three functional LANs. There is a DMZ, a corporate LAN for devices supporting the operations of the organization such as a CEO and IT staff, as well as a LAN segmented off for the lawyers, legal aids, and customer information. Using the example of a law office allows for there to exist data and devices that, if compromised, could cripple or bring ruin to the organization. In this example, it would be confidential attorney–client privileged information from cases that would be treated as lethal compromises. The three different networks had different IP addresses, host names, user names, and domain names to appear unique to assessors and attackers, but the networks were set up identically.

One network was left unchanged as a control. The second network was assessed by an experienced penetration tester and former red team member from a machine in the DMZ using typical offensive security assessment tools and processes. This test was conducted with a scope of assessing the entire organization if possible. The third network was assessed in the CAPTR team methodology, the assessor was made to understand the intent of such an assessment and was given an initial scope of those items that would be lethal to the organization if compromised. This consisted of the case files and the servers they were stored on. These assessors then provided recommendations based on their findings. These recommendations allow for a comparison between what was identified and recommended from traditional security assessment and what was recommended by the CAPTR team resulting in a measure of uniqueness.

Lab Design

With the type of organization decided, the lab network needs to be structured such that it provides for control and realism. The types of technologies involved in the lab network must be as close to representing a real-world organization as possible and the lab must be controlled in a way as to avoid any possible external contamination to the experiment.

Lab Network Operating Systems

The most common operating system in use today is Microsoft Windows (Statistica, 2017) (Net Marketshare, 2017) and the version that is most common is Windows 7 (W3Counter, 2017) (Computer Hope, 2017) (Merriman, 2016). Therefore, the bulk of the lab network will consist of Windows 7 user devices in a domain with Windows 2008 domain controllers, as that is the closest kernel version to Windows 7 for a Windows server operating system. As a note of accountability, at the time of experiment design as well as during the offensive security assessments and simulated attacks, the remote code exploit for these kernel versions, MS17-010 (Microsoft, 2017), also referred to as ETERNALBLUE (Ullrich, 2017), had not been disclosed to the public or weaponized yet and did not impact the carrying out of this experiment.

The network required several Linux-based operating systems as well. As Ubuntu was the most popular and common Linux operating system (Hoffman, 2014), it was chosen to represent Linux platforms in the network. Another Linux distribution, Vyos (Vyos, 2018), was chosen as a routing and firewall platform for the experiment, given its proven history, administration support community, and reliability.

Lab Network Layout

As discussed earlier, the network was intended to be set up representing a law firm network. This required having multiple functional areas for the network as well as allowing communication between them and to the simulated Internet. The network would not connect to the actual Internet to avoid experiment contamination. In Figure 5-1, the three routing devices were using the Vyos operating system, the Internet, and intranet FTP servers, and Case Files Backup were using the Ubuntu operating system and the rest of the machines shown were using Microsoft Windows 7 or Server 2008 for desktop and servers, respectively.

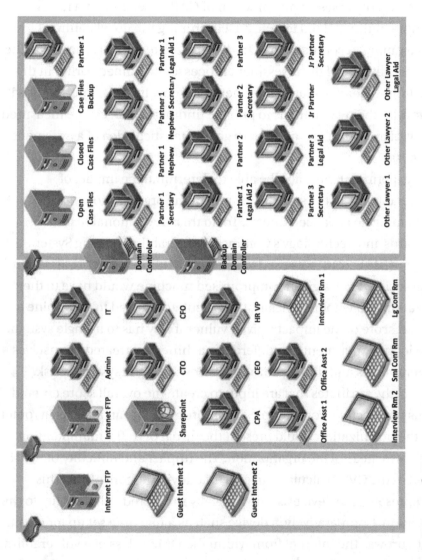

Figure 5-1. Network Diagram

Experiment Metrics

The purpose of this dissertation and experiment are to determine if the offensive security assessment paradigm of CAPTR teaming is a novel augment to traditional red teaming. Determining the novel nature of CAPTR teaming in comparison to traditional red teaming is shown via the categorical analysis of the assessment processes contained earlier in this dissertation. To lend a quantitative metric for novelty, this experiment will also allow for the two methods to provide findings which can be measured in their variance from one another to give a statistical idea of assessment uniqueness.

The experiment must also be able to determine the impact of recommendations to the security posture of the organization and its ability to mitigate advanced threats. To do this, the National Institute of Standards and Technology's Common Vulnerability Scoring System Calculator (NIST, 2018) was used to generate a numerical representation of the associated risk a given compromised machine would have to the organization as a whole. Typically, this calculator is used to determine a numerical score of the impact a given vulnerability has to a single system. For use in the experiment, the different machines are treated themselves as vulnerabilities and the organization is viewed as the system at risk. Therefore, the attributes that are input to create the overall score entered with this perspective. For example, if compromised by an attacker, a router within the organization would present the threat of traffic manipulation between two areas of the organization. The impact and difficulty of which are used in the CVSS calculator to give that device a score of 5.8. This value represents the device as a numerically measured vulnerability to the organization. Comparatively, a device such as a machine set up for clients to use to browse the Internet from within the DMZ is less of a vulnerability to the organization if compromised and represents a lower risk value of 3.4. This is based on the impact and difficulty of turning a compromise of this machine against the organization. The lethal compromise devices within the organization are rated within the CVSS calculator to indicate the difficulty of turning the vulnerability of their compromise against the organization. This was done to include them within the overall risk value for the organization, even though, as lethal compromise items, their compromise would be exponentially critical in comparison to other devices.

Personnel Requirements

To provide as defensible an experiment, the performance of actions in the experiment needs to reflect expected behavior of such actors in the real world. To accomplish this, qualified personnel must be identified to perform the duties of the different actors within the experiment. Additionally, similarly qualified personnel will be identified to audit the actions of the individuals within the experiment to insure nothing is being done outside the bounds of normal activity. The following list indicates the personnel required to facilitate the experimental evaluation of the CAPTR team concept in comparison to that of traditional red teaming:

Systems Administrator

Systems Administration Auditor

Red Teamer

Red Team Auditor

CAPTR Teamer

CAPTR Team Auditor

Qualified and Sophisticated Attacker

Experiment Schedule and Walkthrough

The following is a list indicating the chronological series of events that are required for successful completion of this experiment. Following this list is an in-depth walk-through featuring the details of each phase of the experiment.

1. Control Network and related documentation created by Systems Administrator

2. Control Network audited for realism and functionality by Systems Administration Auditor

3. Control Network cloned twice by Systems Administrator and clone documentation created

4. Red Teamer assesses Network Clone 1

5. Red Team Auditor verifies the Red Teamer recommendations

6. Systems Administration Auditor verifies Red Teamer recommendations

7. Systems Administrator implements changes to Network Clone 1 based on Red Teamer recommendations

8. Red Teamer verifies changes were done in accordance with intent of Red Teamer recommendations

9. CAPTR Teamer assesses Network Clone 2

10. CAPTR Team Auditor verifies the CAPTR Teamer recommendations

11. Systems Administration Auditor verifies CAPTR Teamer recommendations

12. Systems Administrator implements changes to Network Clone 2 based on CAPTR Teamer recommendations

13. CAPTR Teamer verifies changes were done in accordance with intent of CAPTR Teamer recommendations

14. Red Teamer recommendations and CAPTR Teamer recommendations analyzed to indicate novelty metric of CAPTR team process

15. Simulated Attacker wages campaigns against Control Network, Network Clone 1, Network Clone 2

16. Metrics compiled to indicate mitigation of risk to organization in each campaign

Control Network and Related Documentation Created

The systems administrator creates a virtualized lab network in the image of one that could be utilized by a law firm. Devices within the network are configured and domains set up as well as user and administrative accounts. Documentation of the passwords, accounts, and device addresses is compiled. This lab network and its documentation will act as the control network for the experiment as it will simply have a functional level of configuration and no further security measures or alterations of configuration besides that which allow for intended communication and activity.

Network Audited for Realism and Functionality

The Systems Administration Auditor will go over the network
documentation as well as network diagrams of the control network
to determine if it is realistic and indicative of a functional network
configuration. The network will also be audited with regard to its potential
to skew the results of the experiment.

Control Network Cloned

The systems administrator will clone the now verified control network
twice. This is to provide two separate swim lanes for the offensive security
assessment paradigms to work within. The topology, types, and number of
devices will remain identical to the control network. The hostnames, users,
accounts, passwords, and IP addresses of the devices contained within the
clones will be unique for each clone and separate as will the IP schemes
themselves. This is to make them appear as unique as possible come the
attack simulation portion of the experiment.

Red Team Assessment

One of the clone networks will be assessed in the traditional red team
method by the Red Teamer. The assessment of this network will be done
in a time window of ten hours to insure both assessments are concluded
in equal time frames. The Red teamer will then provide recommendations
based on the assessment findings.

Audit of Red Team Recommendations by Red Team Auditor

The recommendations of the Red Teamer are subjected to audit by a Red Team Auditor who is a separate qualified red team practitioner. This is to insure the recommendations from the Red Teamer fall within the scope of expected traditional red team assessment.

Audit of Red Team Recommendations by Systems Administration Auditor

The recommendations of the Red Teamer are further subject to audit by the Systems Administration Auditor. This is done to ensure that the changes suggested by the Red Teamer fall within the scope of activity a typical systems administrator would conduct and not outside the realm of realism.

Implementation of Red Team Recommendations

The Systems Administrator takes the verified recommendations of the Red Teamer and begins implementing them into the Clone 1 network using up to twenty hours of administration time. The Red Teamer is instructed to provide recommendations in an order of importance for implementation and are informed that the Systems Administrator will only have 20 hours to complete the changes to the network. This is done to keep the offensive security assessors from recommending varying amounts of changes for the security of the network which could skew results.

Verification of Red Teamer Recommended Changes

The Red Teamer is also responsible for auditing the implementation of changes conducted by the Systems Administrator based on recommendations of the offensive security assessment. The Red Teamer is to ensure that the changes were performed satisfactorily with regard to the intention of the Red Teamer. This prevents the Systems Administrator from poorly representing the assessment capabilities of the Red Teamer.

CAPTR Team Assessment

The CAPTR Teamer assesses Clone 2 of the control network. This is done in the same allotted time as the ten hours given to the Red Teamer. The CAPTR Teamer is sent network documentation and a letter indicating the spirit of the CAPTR team to the CAPTR teamer as well as scope and rules for the engagement. Recommendation guidelines are sent to the CAPTR teamer as well. The CAPTR Teamer will provide recommendations based on findings of the offensive security assessment.

Audit of CAPTR Team Recommendations by CAPTR Team Auditor

Similar to the recommendations of the red team, those of the CAPTR team are also audited by a separate party who is also qualified in offensive security and given the same intent of CAPTR team's information as the CAPTR Teamer. This will allow for third party verification that the changes suggested by this assessment method are in keeping within the spirit of CAPTR teaming.

Audit of CAPTR Team Recommendations by Systems Administration Auditor

Also, like the Red Team recommendations, those of the CAPTR team are subject to the same audit by the Systems Administration Auditor to determine that they fall within the scope of activity a typical systems administrator can be expected to perform.

Implementation of CAPTR Team Changes

The Systems Administrator takes the verified recommendations of the CAPTR Teamer and begins implementing them into the Clone 2 network also using up to twenty hours of administration time. The CAPTR Teamer is also instructed to provide recommendations in an order of importance for implementation and are informed that the Systems Administrator will only have 20 hours to complete the changes to the network. The Systems Administrator will provide a log of changes implemented into the Clone 2 network to the CAPTR Teamer.

Verification of CAPTR Teamer Recommended Changes

The CAPTR Teamer is also responsible for auditing the implementation of changes conducted by the Systems Administrator based on recommendations of the offensive security assessment. The CAPTR Teamer is to ensure that the changes were performed satisfactorily with regard to the intention of the CAPTR Teamer. This prevents the Systems Administrator from poorly representing the assessment capabilities of the CAPTR Teamer.

Recommended Changes Analyzed

The changes suggested by the two teams are compared to indicate whether or not the two offensive security assessment paradigms provided the same or different results. This is part of the basis for making the case that the CAPTR team paradigm is a worthwhile augment to established techniques. If the changes recommended by either team were nearly identical it would make a weak statement for the novelty of CAPTR teaming. If the changes were largely different then there is a stronger case for the paradigm.

Simulated Attacks

Cyber-attack campaigns are conducted against the control and clone networks. The Attacker is instructed to replicate motivated and sophisticated attacks against the organization in each of the three campaigns. The Attacker is informed that the organization for all three campaigns are legal firms and that the goal is to compromise as much of the network as possible with the specific goal of finding case files as they are the item of lethal compromise for these organizations. The attacker is given a maximum of 40 hours to conduct each of the cyber-attacks from the access provided, which is as earlier discussed, a user context implant running as if by successful spear phishing. The order of the campaigns is unknown to the attacker; however, the Control was attacked first, the Red

Team secured network second, and the CAPTR team secured network third. This was to ensure that if the Attacker gained any proficiency as the attack campaigns were completed that the attacks would be most proficient against the CAPTR team secured network, and any bias this created would make attacks against the CAPTR Team network most likely to be successful and, if anything, skew results against the CAPTR team model.

Metrics Compiled

Once the campaigns are completed, the compromised devices are tallied and a percentage of the overall risk present in the network secured is identified for each. This is done to provide a quantitative measure of the amount of risk mitigated by the changes recommended by the offensive security assessments.

Addressing Defensibility Requirements

Briefly, this section summarizes ways in which the aforementioned experiment is able to address the requisite characteristics for defensibility. The virtualized lab simulation of a network serving as a replica of potential real network servicing a law firm means that it is both controlled and a realistic situation to conduct both offensive security assessment and attack simulation. Further, the great lengths taken to guarantee remote communication of actors while maintaining a contaminant-free experiment mean that no outside actor or incident will affect the lab network.

Addressing Defensible Security Assessments

Using a lab network not connected to the Internet means that security assessment is conducted in a vacuum, free of user- and administrator-created events that may unfairly help or hinder one assessment methodology over the other. The use of industry-qualified offensive security experts in the carrying out of the assessments provides both defensibility to their assessment as well as furthering realism. Additionally, having the assessments audited by similarly qualified separate third-party offensive security experts means there is an extra level of validation for the legitimacy of the assessments and the generated recommendations provided from them. The equal limit of time and like recommendation guidelines means that both assessment paradigms have fair assessment engagement windows and know the time restrictions on the administrator ahead of time.

Addressing Defensible Systems Administration

Ensuring the networks were created and administered across the separate assessment platforms by the same administrator insured that one network did not receive more or less qualified systems administration than the other. The audit of the networks themselves by a separate third-party qualified systems administrator prevented the lab network from failing to represent a realistic operating environment. The audit of the assessment recommendations from both teams by a third-party systems administrator insured that the implementations needed were within the scope of typical systems administration and would not skew the outcome of the test in favor of one assessment paradigm over the other. The equal limit of time for change implementation across both assessed networks kept the implementation of security fair between both assessed networks. Lastly, the presentation of change logs regarding the assessor recommendations back to the assessor insured that the changes done to the networks were in keeping with the intention of the assessors.

The use of an extremely qualified cyber operations expert and senior red team member with experience performing APT emulation allowed for an equal level of sophistication to be applied to all three attack campaigns. The level of skill maintained by the attacker meant that the networks were more likely to see deeper assessment penetration and therefore changes recommended by the assessors were more likely to face attacker scrutiny. Having a simulated attacker means that no outside attackers could influence the emulation campaigns and, therefore, it would be similarly capable of targeting each of the three networks. The brief to the attacker on specific motivation for the legal firm's case files, in addition to wanting the whole network compromised, meant that the actor had a distinct purpose that was the same for all three networks, which achieved a fair level of motivation in all three campaigns.

Addressing Measurable Results

The comparison of number of recommendations and their uniqueness between the two evaluated assessment paradigms allowed for a measure of novelty between the suggested CAPTR Team paradigm and established red team practices. Utilization of the NIST-provided CVSS calculator to calculate the risk each compromised machine allowed for a comparable quantitative evaluation metric. This allowed the experiment to grade the success of the paradigms in protecting overall risk as well as the ability to directly compare the paradigms to each other.

Summary

The information technology industry is really good at benchmarking and evaluating newer and better security hardware or software, but not so much "wetware" (humans). That fact is problematic for innovation in industry and, I suspect, is probably the largest reason academic innovation mostly avoids research into human-driven cybersecurity implementation assessment processes. I can easily prove my encryption technique is better if it has less overhead or makes data more secure. I can readily show how my software alerts on more data than existing products. It is really hard to show my cybersecurity implementation stands up to the human-involved attack tradecraft and human-involved operations. This chapter presented defensibility requirements for experimentally comparing cybersecurity implementations against each other. It also touched on the high level of difficulty and the dire need for continued improvement if we are going to push the envelope on theoretical cybersecurity.

CHAPTER 6

Strategic Cybersecurity

Strategic cybersecurity is accomplished through orienting every facet of cybersecurity efforts, expenditures, technologies, and personnel toward the immediate and long-term strategic goals and outcomes of the organization they protect. Imagine you were the Chief Information Security Officer (CISO) or otherwise in control of the cybersecurity apparatus of an organization. Let's say this organization is a sneaker company. You get called into the CEO's office and she is sitting there with the entire board and ownership of the sneaker company. She looks you in the eye and she tells you this:

> Your budget for the next year will be five million dollars. I want you to spend it on cybersecurity things that will enable me to sell the most sneakers possible. I do not care if we get hacked, how bad we get hacked, or even who or what in the company gets hacked. I just want to profit as much from sneaker sales as possible year over year and continue operation for as long as possible and those are the only measure that I will evaluate you on moving forward.

© Dr. Jacob G. Oakley, Michael Butler, Wayne York, Dr. Matthew Puckett, Dr. J. Louis Sewell 2022
J. G. Oakley et al., *Theoretical Cybersecurity*, https://doi.org/10.1007/978-1-4842-8300-4_6

OK wow, that would be quite the statement from organizational leadership, but what if it happened? What would that look like? What would you do with that challenge? The answer, in whatever form you give it, would be strategic cybersecurity. This is because in response to such a challenge, any solution given would be aimed at improving the strategic outcome of the sneaker company, profit as much as possible from sneaker sales and operate for as long as possible.

There are a lot of ways to approach this challenge from a cybersecurity perspective and a lot of novel ways to implement cybersecurity solutions. Maybe, as the CISO, you decide to focus on profit by minimizing downtime. Maybe we focus on longevity by protecting the trade secrets of our shoe company. The thing is, if, as an industry, we can be successful at strategic cybersecurity, we will not only improve the totality of our body of work, but we will also improve external support for our efforts and appear as an enabler and not as a tax or cost that an organization or its operational units must pay.

As we have just discussed, the areas and aspects of an organizational attack surface we choose to focus on are as numerous as the threats faced. Since they are largely tailored to the specific organization, I will not waste time trying to exhaustively compile a list of cybersecurity problems to tackle that are directly tied to strategic cybersecurity. Instead, we will walk through several cybersecurity implementations that are strategic in nature, regardless of what type of organization they are applied to simply because of their methodologies and implementations.

What It Is Not

Since the term cybersecurity strategy is a well-known and possibly overused one, I just wanted to take a moment to point out that it is vastly different than strategic cybersecurity. Cybersecurity strategy is a near and long-term plan to achieve cybersecurity outcomes and goals, which do not necessarily align directly with an organization's own strategic mission.

A Move Toward Resiliency

Our sneaker company example certainly plants the seeds of theoretical cybersecurity exploration. We can easily see that there are many ways we could change the way we look at cybersecurity as an industry and a body of work if we had this kind of organizational support. My stance is that we are currently at the infancy of this sort of process, and it will require a lot of evolution in thinking and is probably generational in forming. We need to change a lot of bias about threats, cybersecurity, and how we view being networked and on the Internet in general for statements anywhere near like our fictitious CEO said to be commonplace.

Still, I think there has been a subconscious shift to address the lack of strategic cybersecurity in the vast growth in cybersecurity resiliency technologies, businesses, approaches, and efforts. As a society and industry, we are beginning to realize the basic truth that if someone really wants to hack you, they eventually will and that there are too many threats with too much variance to completely mitigate for any organization. Therefore, the natural response is to not focus less on stopping every attack but more on coping with as much damage as possible. This lets you be threat agnostic and focus more on things an organization does know in the things it can't live without, how long it can survive in various circumstances, etc.

Resilience in this sense and efforts and technologies to improve it are certainly strategic in nature since they are based on knowledge about the organizations ability to operate and not so much on what threats exist. In my mind this shift is extremely valuable to our industry and to our customers as it leaves less room for showmanship, lying, and bamboozling through scare tactics so common at conferences, tradeshows, and websites of cybersecurity vendors. Instead of trying to scare a customer into buying protection from APTs who are probably never going to bother targeting them in the first place, let's start helping our customers weather as many storms and as fierce of storms as we can and not sell hurricane insurance to companies in Switzerland and stop marketing avalanche prevention services to companies in Australia.

On Cybersecurity Insurance

Since I have spent much of this book atop my tower of soap boxes, I think we can throw one more on the pile. It feels it is important to point out the problem that cybersecurity insurance poses. It may seem like a natural fit for strategic cybersecurity and an improvement to resilience. And why not? Insurance lets an organization simply buy down risk with predictable dollars by shifting less predictable risk and expenditures it to an insurer. So, what's the problem?

It turns out there are a few. Firstly, any time you mix both technical jargon and legal jargon, the opportunity for misunderstanding, misinterpreting, or misrepresentation is extremely high. If you are an organization that doesn't feel strongly enough about your cybersecurity competencies that you want to just buy down risk through insurance instead of fixing it though technology, policy, and people, do you really think you would be able to articulate the technical arguments necessary when the insuring organization says you didn't live up to the requirements necessary to maintain coverage for a given hack?

That and other problems with cybersecurity insurance to the customer aside, there is also the issue of the attackers. In normal insurance, there is certainly insurance fraud and there is also a long history of enforcement and protections put in place. When you try to insure against cybersecurity attacks, and specifically ransomware and ransoms though, aren't we in a way encouraging the attackers as well as informing them on the right amount of ransom to request to result in payout most likely? This line of questioning has been explored by others in our profession more experienced and widely known than myself, and all of it so far has been interesting reading. I just wanted to touch on it in this chapter since I think it is a natural progression of thought along the lines of strategic cybersecurity and its manifestation in general terms through a shift toward resiliency.

Counter-APT Red Teaming

Counter-APT Red Teaming or CAPTR Teaming is a strategic offensive cybersecurity paradigm that leverages outcome-oriented scoping, criticality-supported initialization perspectives and reverse red teaming methodologies to strategically implement pro-active, offensive cybersecurity assessment. This theoretical cybersecurity idea was one I proposed, experimented on, and validated for my doctoral dissertation and is covered ad nauseum in that document and to a detailed degree on the book *Professional Red Teaming* as well. The following is enough of an introduction to the concept to illustrate an example of how strategic cybersecurity can show up in the offensive cybersecurity sector of our industry. The following chapter will have more defensive oriented example material on how strategic cybersecurity might be incorporated on the blue side of things in support of an organization's strategic goals and outcomes.

Outcome-Oriented Scoping

The identification of scope by the CAPTR team is a multi-part process focused on identifying those items that pose lethal or critical impact if compromised. The scope in a CAPTR team assessment is intended to allow assessment resources to home in on a limited and prioritized subset of the overall organization. Scoping the assessment this way is necessary if the selected initial assessment assets are to enable the CAPTR team engagement to be successful. The scope of a CAPTR team engagement is more outcome-oriented than in a traditional red team assessment as productivity and cost benefit are directly tied to appropriate identification of critical or lethal compromise items that meet the threshold for inclusion. This is done by using appropriate personnel to perform worst-case scenario risk assessment, centrality analysis, and adequate prioritization of potential targets.

Worst-Case Risk Assessment

Traditionally, in risk management and asset prioritization, the leadership of an organization will use a standard risk matrix to determine which items present the highest risk (the bolded regions in Figure 6-1) and to address those first.

Likelihood/consequence	Risk				
	Not significant	Minor	Moderate	Major	Critical
Almost certain	Medium	High	**Very high**	**Very high**	**Very high**
Likely	Medium	High	**High**	**Very high**	**Very high**
Possible	Low	Medium	High	High	**Very high**
Unlikely	Low	Low	Medium	Medium	High
Rare	Low	Low	Low	Low	Medium

Figure 6-1. *Red Team Risk Focus*

The CAPTR team helps the organization leadership understand that the likelihood does not matter for critical or lethal items and to assume compromise is possible and probable. This is done to afford the greatest mitigation of advanced threat actor activity. If an APT is intent on targeting such items within the organization, it is only a matter of time until these items will be at risk. This should move risk prioritization toward addressing those items that fall in the critical column of a typical risk matrix such as in Figure 6-2 (bolded regions), as the worst case is assumed and the likelihood of attempted and eventually successful compromise by an APT is accepted to be almost certain.

Likelihood/consequence	Risk				
	Not significant	Minor	Moderate	Major	Critical
Almost certain	Medium	High	Very high	Very high	**Very high**
Likely	Medium	High	High	Very High	**Very high**
Possible	Low	Medium	High	High	**Very high**
Unlikely	Low	Low	Medium	Medium	**High**
Rare	Low	Low	Low	Low	**Medium**

Figure 6-2. *CAPTR Team Risk Focus*

Survivability

Essentially, the question being asked in CAPTR team scoping is, what losses can this organization not afford to sustain. Determining the correct answer to that question involves all facets of the customer organization as well as the offensive security expertise maintained by assessors. Much like in traditional red teaming, the operational as well as security or infrastructure-oriented staff are needed to appropriately identify the scope. One immediately identifiable difference is the inclusion of the offensive security professionals in developing the needed scope. As we discussed earlier, typically, the scope is defined by the customer before the assessment and it acts as more of a constraint than an enabling attribute of the engagement. There is also a specific order to the involvement of personnel as well since the shaping of a CAPTR scope is an evolving process that ends with asset prioritization and a risk apogee.

CAPTR Team Critical Initialization Perspective

As outlined, the CAPTR team's use of critical perspective starts at a point or points of presence that are identified as posing the greatest risk to the organization. The focus of an assessment from this perspective is to

107

identify vulnerabilities local to such devices that would enable an attacker to compromise the critical item. The assessment can then be expanded to the points in the organization that would allow an attacker to pivot to the critical items and continues outward. This fourth perspective is aimed at mitigating the impact of a breach regardless of its source. No matter the vulnerability that allowed an attacker in or the locality of an insider threat should affect this assessment perspective. Beginning security assessments at the goal of a compromise instead of assessing the potential starting points provides an enhanced ability to mitigate a myriad of threats. This perspective differs from the internal initialization perspective in that it starts at the CAPTR team scope-identified points of lethal or critical compromise, not simply an unspecific privileged or unprivileged access within the organization. This critical initialization perspective is illustrated in Figure 6-3.

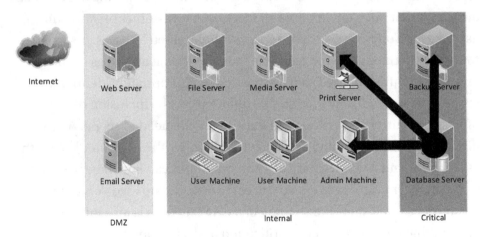

Figure 6-3. *Critical Initialization Perspective*

This differs from traditional attacks that are more likely to begin from external perspectives or internal unprivileged perspectives resulting from attacks like spear phishing which are shown in Figures 6-4 and 6-5, respectively.

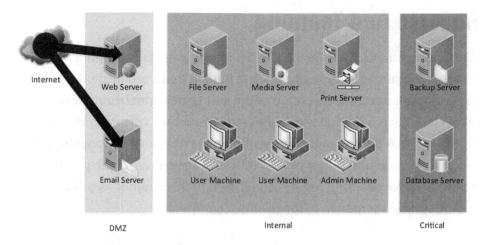

Figure 6-4. *External Initialization Perspective*

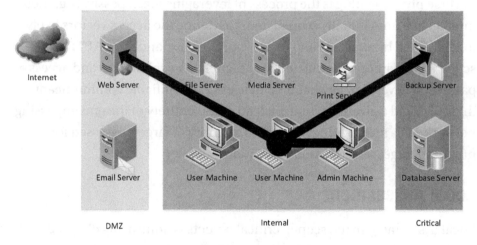

Figure 6-5. *Internal Initialization Perspective*

Reverse Red Teaming

With the targets selected via the CAPTR teaming-specific scoping methodology and the most appropriate launch point established using the critical perspective, execution of the assessment can begin. Reverse pivot chaining is a unique way of assessing from the critical perspective that creates a reporting mechanism utilizing reverse risk relationships to provide extremely high-cost benefit to such engagements. The process of reverse pivot chaining will be established in this chapter as will the benefits and presentation of the results it can yield.

Reverse Pivot Chaining

Reverse pivot chaining is the process of leveraging local, passively gathered intelligence from initially scoped items to define the access vectors likely to be utilized by attackers and to appropriately expand the CAPTR team scope toward improving efficiency of higher risk exploitation and access pathways. Reverse pivot chaining focuses on identifiable communicants that surround a given machine instead of the entirety of the encompassing network. This methodology sacrifices quantity of targets assessed for precision target selection and evaluation.

Local Assessment

Local assessment of the scoped critical objects is done using elevated privilege under the assumption that an APT could eventually achieve such context during a compromise. Local privilege escalation vulnerabilities and local misconfigurations that would allow an attacker to ultimately affect the confidentiality, integrity, or availability of the compromise object are assessed at the very onset of the CAPTR team engagement window. Further, this local context is used to identify potential remote access vectors such as code execution exploits or poor authentication configurations. With access to locally stored data and operating system functions, the CAPTR team assessor can efficiently identify access vectors an attacker would use against the initially scoped items without having to perform potentially risky blind scanning and exploitation.

The best way to underscore the benefits of this method are through a simple example using the following network. CAPTR teaming's outcome-oriented scoping defined the Linux file server constitutes a lethal compromise to the organization, and assessment will be carried out using the critical initialization perspective of starting with access to the server as shown in Figure 6-6.

Figure 6-6. *CAPTR Team Assessment Directionality*

After running several situation awareness commands, much like those covered in the operational best practices chapter, the assessors have use of locally available, native operating system commands to determine much about the machine deemed as a lethal compromise object in the organization.

The assessor has learned that the kernel version used by the Linux server is out of date and vulnerable to a local privilege escalation vulnerability. the ability to transition from an unprivileged user to a super user on such a critical machine in the organization constitutes an extremely dangerous risk. This risk is also one that would have gone undiscovered in other assessment models had they not completely and successfully compromised devices in the network leading to and including this machine, which could potentially reside deep within a target organization. CAPTR teaming immediately assessed the lethal compromise item and, within the first few moments of establishing situational awareness, found a critical reportable item without even proceeding to outward exploitation and expansion of the assessment.

Initial situational awareness commands also informed the assessor that there were three machines communicating with the lethal compromise item. There was one computer, presumably an administrator, which was found to be using SSH to remotely access and administer the box. This information was found on the filesystem itself. Logs and files related to the SSH protocol were found in the user's directory on the machine, and the user's activity in the command history of the device showed activity typical of an administrator. Without the local privileged perspective used in CAPTR teaming, this information may have never been discovered, and if it had, it meant that typical red team assessment had remotely exploited several devices as well as having run a potentially dangerous kernel-level privilege escalation exploit to get privileges to view the same information that the CAPTR methodology began with.

The established connections to the machine that the assessors identified through native operating system commands indicated the presence of the other two communicants. One was accessing a read-only web file share on port 80 that the Linux server was hosting and the other was accessing a file transfer server on port 21. Further inspection led the assessors to identify that the file transfer server was used to put files on to the Linux server for other users to view and download. Through further local intelligence gathering, the assessors also found that the file transfer ability was not limited to a specific location such as the web file share directory and that a remote file transfer could overwrite several unprotected scripts that were being executed with superuser privileges by the machines scheduling mechanism.

No exploitation has been performed, and we already have the following extremely valuable findings to report upon within less than a day of assessment:

- Local privilege escalation using kernel exploit

- Remote code execution as superuser due to:

    - Poorly configured permissions of world writeable scheduled jobs being executed as superuser

    - Unconstrained file transfer server.

Analysis of Local Intelligence

The assessment has also identified the three tier one communicants of the lethal compromise item. With these targets identified, the CAPTR team must perform analysis to identify which order to conduct assessment of these hosts. This prioritization is also valuable to the reporting that will come later in identifying which links are most dangerous. These risk links are constituted by the source, the destination, and the method and privilege of communication. It is possible to have multiple links between devices. For example, if the admin machine could access the lethal compromise by either SSH as an admin user or file transfer as an unprivileged user it would mean that an attacker needs less privilege gained on that tier one communicant to then attack the lethal compromise object. As we continue on this example, I am only providing some simple decision points for prioritization and assessment. Each actual scenario will impose its own unique attributes to any offensive security assessment and the decisions of the assessors may drive the engagement differently. This scenario should clarify the process and not be taken as guidance on how exactly to make risk-based decisions, as all risks and every organization vary.

The risk links identified via local assessment of our scoped lethal compromise item are shown in Figure 6-7 and listed as follows:

- Superuser on 10.0.0.2 can access 10.0.0.1 as superuser using the SSH protocol

- Unprivileged user on 10.0.0.3 can access 10.0.0.1 as an unprivileged user using FTP

- Unprivileged user on 10.0.0.4 can access 10.0.0.1 as an unprivileged user using HTTP

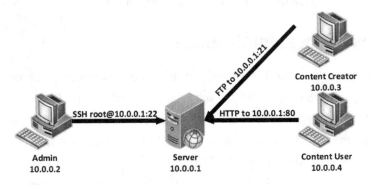

Figure 6-7. Communication Links

The first risk link constitutes the most risk to the lethal compromise item as it provides immediate interactive access as a superuser to the lethal compromise item. Any attacker able to compromise that tier one communicant poses grave danger to the Linux server. The FTP link is ranked second as it provides unprivileged access; however, it also allows for files to be moved to the lethal compromise server, and given what we know about the identified local privilege escalation vulnerabilities that are present, it is a potential, yet more complicated path to remote interaction. The HTTP link is last because it is a read only ability for unprivileged users to download data from the privileged host and would require leveraging of an additional risk link to pose much danger to the lethal compromise item.

Reverse Pivoting

At this point, the assessors have established a prioritized list of targets which will be rolled into the scope of the CAPTR assessment. These targets will be assessed remotely for potential access vectors and vulnerabilities using well-known or custom scanning and exploitation tools. Any successfully compromised tier one communicant will then be subject to the same local intelligence gathering that was performed on the lethal compromise item, but with one difference. In addition to identifying information related to remote communicants that may access the device, it is also analyzed as its ability to be a spreader. In this sense, both outside in, and inside out communication pathways become valuable to the CAPTR team assessors.

We have initially identified the admin machine as the highest risk link to the lethal compromise item, but what if, upon reverse pivoting, it is identified that the machine used for content creation, which FTPs to the lethal compromise server is accessible by ten other machines and it has a remote code vulnerability of its own. Further, it is administered using the same account and source machine as the lethal compromise site. As such, any successful access and privilege escalation on the content creation box would lead an attacker to gain the superuser credentials due to the key being stored for convenience on the device. The other two tier one communicants were not found to have remote access vulnerabilities so certainly the content creation machine should now be considered the highest risk within the organization.

The chaining together of this iterative reverse pivot process allows the assessor's to surgically establish a web of risk relationships and identify attributes of those communicants that may prioritize them as attack vectors. It is also important to remember that CAPTR teaming is another tool in the chest for offensive security practitioners. It does not assess the whole network a lethal compromise item resides in, but it is a focus on likely communication paths. Also, it is important to remember that many advanced attackers are likely to do their best to blend in with and leverage established communication methods to achieve compromise. The extremely efficient focus on those items specifically lends credibility to this CAPTR process even though its methodology is a reversal of traditional red team and attacker directionality.

CAPTR Reporting

Using the previous example as an analogy for actual targets which may be much larger, it should be readily apparent that the reverse pivot chaining process will result in a web of risk links between hosts that converge on the lethal compromise item(s) established by the outcome-oriented scoping. One of the benefits of this methodology is the safety that can be maintained by the assessing party. In fact, a CAPTR team assessment need not exploit a single vulnerability to be extremely effective. In a high-risk environment where traditionally red team activity is frowned upon due to the risk it introduces, CAPTR teaming can be a great alternative. Instead of attempting remote exploitation of tier one communicants, the assessors could simply use administrative access provided by the host organization to perform the local intelligence gathering on each tier one communicant to identify their capability as a spreader and which devices further out in the network act as tier two communicants. Though this method lacks the proof of concept of actual exploitation, it can be efficiently and safely be performed by assessors with the attacker mindset and skill set to the benefit of the host organization.

Web of Reverse Risk Relationships

Accumulation of the risk link data throughout the engagement allows for a logical representation of the web of risk relationships in the organization that lead back to the initially scoped items. In earlier chapters, we discussed that the CAPTR scope may consist of several devices. The same logic is applicable and local assessment can be performed on them in a prioritized order, the tier one communicants are just made up of the total list of hosts that communicate to any or one of the initially scoped items. Here specifically, the ability to be a spreader is important as any tier one communicant, or even initially scoped item for that matter, that communicates with multiple lethal or critical compromise items in the initial scope becomes an elevated risk. Though logical in nature, the web or reverse risk relationships can easily be turned into a graphical representation of organizational risk capable of communicating to even non-technical managers where the focus of the organization security apparatus should be. As the web becomes bigger, it also allows an organization a unique view at cumulative risk cardinality. The identified risk of a given machine or a reverse link to the lethal compromise item and thus the greater organization is continually evolved through the engagement as tiers of communicants are assessed and the aggregation of links to significant spreaders and higher risk items becomes apparent.

Math Is Hard

I will touch on this because I think an organization deciding to undergo CAPTR team assessment could also tailor the results to be extremely useful in a quantitative analysis of risk relating to the initially scoped items. I am no math whiz, but a definition of weight for the risk posed by having a given amount of communication links, vulnerabilities, and capability as a spreader could certainly lead to mathematical analysis and representation of the web of reverse risk relationships and the cumulative risk cardinality of machines. The reason I did not provide what I think this would look like is because it should be different for every organization. When possible, though, taking the CAPTR process and applying metrics to quantitatively establish risk using the results could be invaluable to addressing organization risk that comes from critical or lethal compromise items.

A Discussion on CAPTR Reporting Cost Benefit

Identifying potential vulnerabilities that are present to the lethal threats within an organization by leveraging less resources in an expedited assessment window is the apex of the CAPTR team concept. Prioritization of initially scoped compromise items and then the efficient assessment of those items and their communicants using the CAPTR team method represents a widely applicable cost benefit over traditional assessment methods. The reporting mechanism enabled by the relational risk data the CAPTR assessment gathers regarding initially scoped items and paths of potential access to them enables security and monitoring teams. Further, non-technical management is empowered to make cost-effective, security-related budget decisions utilizing the risk link web. As an example, candidates of CAPTR team assessment, take the organizational diagram in Figure 6-8.

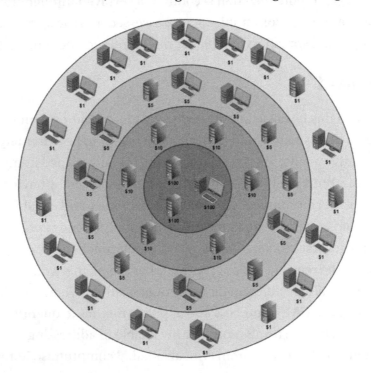

Figure 6-8. *Organization Object Risk Values*

This is a diagram of organizational resources separated into bands based on their cost to the organization if compromised. This is a simplified depiction and the US dollar is simply representative currency of the risk value the objects have to the organization. There are three objects with a risk value of $100, six with a risk value of $10, 12 with a risk value of $5, and 18 with a risk value of $1. The total risk value for all the objects in the organization is $438.

Figure 6-9 shows overlays of the previous diagram showing the likely outcome of scoping for both a CAPTR team engagement and a traditional offensive security engagement such as red teaming or penetration testing.

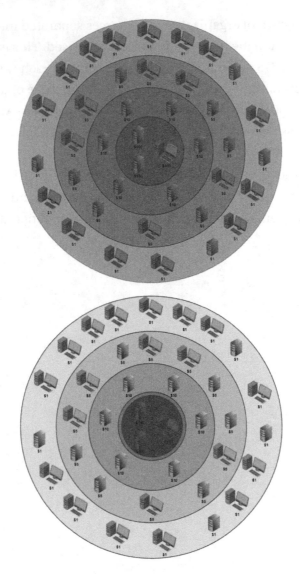

Figure 6-9. *Traditional Offensive Security Scope and CAPTR Team Initial Scope*

On the left is a representation of typical scoping for a traditional offensive security engagement. Since the aim of such engagements is to simulate an attack on an organization in an effort to uncover any weaknesses (Choo et al., 2007), the entire organization is subject to assessment and therefore included in the scope if possible. The CAPTR team scope is limited to items of critical importance which, in this case, are the three objects in the organization with risk values of $100. Although high value items are included in both scopes, it can be certain in the CAPTR team assessment that they will be assessed. In the traditionally scoped engagement, the likelihood that every item is assessed is highly dependent on the assessors' skill and the window of time allotted to the assessors. Next consider the following representations of example findings from both types of engagements.

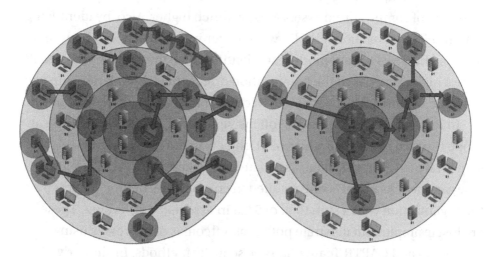

Figure 6-10. *Traditional and CAPTR Team Example Findings*

On the left are example findings resulting from the scope used by traditional offensive security assessments and on the right are the findings resultant from the CAPTR team assessment. The red circles over objects represent their compromise during engagements and the red arrows depict a pivot to another device via information found on the previously assessed host. In an effort to assess weaknesses in the entire organization, the traditional assessment method did compromise one of the high value targets as well as many others. This shows the potential for a traditional assessment to compromise and progress to many hosts within the organization, but perhaps not to all of those identified as being particularly high in value to the organization. Conversely, the scope of the CAPTR team assessment allows for those high value systems to be assessed from an elevated privilege at the onset. This initial scope also leads to the identification of communicating hosts that pose potential access vectors an attacker could take to attack the high value items. Those are then assessed and compromise if possible and the process then continues for the duration of the assessment window. This method potentially compromises fewer hosts than traditional models; however, the value of compromised assets is likely much higher. Also, by identifying communication relationships between lower value objects and high value objects, the CAPTR team model can identify which low value hosts actually pose a high value risk to the organization due to their risk relationship with the critical items in the overall web of compromise carried out by the team.

In Figure 6-10, the traditional offensive security assessment of typical scope resulted in a compromise of 21 objects in the organization with a sum total of $171 in risk value associated with them. The CAPTR team assessment of its initial scope resulted in compromise of nine objects in the organization with a sum total of $323 in associated risk value. These are just examples but illustrate potential outcomes of processes using traditional and CAPTR Team offensive security methods. In similarly timed engagement windows, CAPTR teaming would realistically lead to the assessment and compromise of at least those most valuable items included in its initial scope totaling $300 in risk value. To identify findings with this level of impact, the traditional offensive security assessment would have to go on long enough to engage at least two of the three high value items as well as all others within the organization.

To understand the benefit the CAPTR team process provides in translatable recommendations to host organizations, again consider the CAPTR team example findings in Figure 6-11 shown larger as follows:

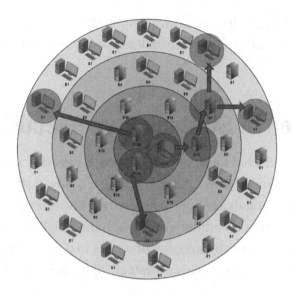

Figure 6-11. *CAPTR Team Example Findings*

The findings in Figure 6-11 will be discovered in an order that reflects their distance from those initially scoped critical items and their different communicants. Findings on the high value items are of grave concern to the organization and should be addressed quickly. The next tier of hosts comprises those that directly communicate with the initially scoped items. In this diagram, for example, an object with a risk value of $1 is found to directly communicate with a high value item from the initial scope. The risk web provided by mapping communicating hosts and their tiered relationship to the critical items allows even non-technical managers to easily understand the value of fixing the identified $1 object. At face value, a vulnerability in a $1 value object may be simply accepted instead of mitigated as part of the risk analysis based on offensive security findings. This is due to the fact that the organization might not view spending $10 to fix a problem on a $1 machine a worthwhile investment of resources. The CAPTR team model, however, represents its results in such a way that the $1 machine vulnerability is actually identified as being a potentially $100 problem due to its relationship with the initially scoped critical items.

Now a potentially unaddressed critical vulnerability is prioritized in a way reflecting its ability to impact the overall risk value associated with an organization.

Application of Strategic Cybersecurity

So we have learned what the concept of strategic cybersecurity is and we have walked through how CAPTR teaming is a way of strategically implementing the practice of offensive security. The following is a contrast between what a traditional approach that might be taken in the application of offensive cybersecurity practices to our example sneaker company compared against using a strategic approach via CAPTR teaming assessment.

The Classic Approach

As outlined in the description of what and why CAPTR team assessments are, we described that in large part, scoping and initialization are points of potential improvement in what would be described as traditional red teaming or penetration testing events. In a classic offensive security application, leveraging such testing, the same would hold true. The CISO of our sneaker company would seek our offensive security assessment to identify potential gaps in their network security posture for improvement. This would likely be done for one of two reasons. Offensive security assessment such as penetration testing may be a regular part of the organization security framework, such as for information assurance certification, or the organization has recently been breached and wants to assess its posture in a post remediation.

Regardless of why such services are procured, the process is essentially a scope of targets, and a timeline is agreed upon between the consumer and producer of the offensive security solution. Typically, the scope, time, and number of resources put on this test will be driven by the CISO's budgetary allocation. This means mileage may vary and if the test is being done to check a box of "yes we have done our annual penetration test or red team event," then the solution is usually focused on how cheaply this can be accomplished. What this usually leads to is short, low-resourced assessments that focus on scoped targets accessible from the external initialization perspective, that is, the organizations external network perimeter. The result is often little findings, and even when vulnerabilities are discovered, they are on systems of lesser consequence or higher replicability due to the nature of them existing on the external side of the organizations security posture. Therefore, a classic approach provides a traditional offensive security assessment whose results are likely to be of little consequence to the organization. In fact, the goal of such assessments is more a function of compliance than for the discovery of actual vulnerabilities.

The Strategic Approach

Using a method like CAPTR teaming allows for even short, low-resourced offensive cybersecurity assessments to be tailored toward providing the most cybersecurity cost benefit with regards to the organization's strategic goals and outcomes. If the onus is on having done an annual penetration test, why not do one that does as much as possible to support the organization's strategic mission?

In this strategic approach, the CISO would go through the outcome-oriented scoping and worst-case risk assessment used for CAPTR teaming. The offensive cybersecurity assessment would then be targeted at critical assets, directly supporting the organization's strategic tasks, and achieving its strategic goals. Since time is not wasted on more trivial externally scoped assets, any findings are likely to be of high consequence and directly inform remediation efforts aimed at protecting strategic assets. In this strategic approach for offensive cybersecurity, CAPTR team assessments would allow or sneaker CISO to not only check the compliance box for having done the annual assessment but potentially finds issues in strategic assets, such as servers running intellectual property like proprietary sneaker design software that gives it a leg up over its competition and allows it to stay in the infinite game longer by protecting such attack surface as a priority through targeted vulnerability assessment of those strategic targets.

Summary

This chapter served as an introduction to the concept of strategic cybersecurity. Examples like that of our shoe company CISO will hopefully become more the norm as theoretical cybersecurity concepts such as strategic cybersecurity are more common. This will only be possible through improvements and encouragements in the cybersecurity industry that result in more theoretical cybersecurity research for the sake of improving cybersecurity and its application. We also covered how the family or sector of cybersecurity that is offensive cybersecurity can be tailored to enable strategic cybersecurity. With unique scoping, initialization perspective, and reverse red teaming methodology, Counter APT Red teaming allows for offensive security to be implemented in a way that is aimed at protecting an organization's strategic goals and outcomes and less on protecting it from every threat.

CHAPTER 7

Strategic Defensive Security

In the previous chapter, we discussed a scenario in which a CISO was given a budget of $5 million to develop the cybersecurity program of a sneaker company. Our CISO has been given a very large task, but before they begin, they need to consider the objective of their security program. The objective may seem obvious, in fact, it is so obvious that it is rarely even considered worth mentioning or debating – don't get hacked! Cybersecurity means preventing the bad guys from getting in, so this program should do just that, right?

This is what I would consider the classical approach to a cybersecurity program. This principle has been the core of the cybersecurity conversation for decades, with CISOs and their security personnel attempting to prevent any sort of compromise across their organization. Resources are spread wide, security solutions deployed equally on every host, and analysts watch for any sign of compromise across thousands of network points, turning cybersecurity into a vast game of whack-a-mole played at the speed of processors.

But before we go down the road of the classical approach to cybersecurity, perhaps we should take a moment to learn the lesson that cybersecurity has been trying to teach us for decades – it doesn't matter what technology you use, how many highly skilled security personnel you employ, or how locked down your policies are, you will get hacked.

© Dr. Jacob G. Oakley, Michael Butler, Wayne York, Dr. Matthew Puckett, Dr. J. Louis Sewell 2022   127
J. G. Oakley et al., *Theoretical Cybersecurity*, https://doi.org/10.1007/978-1-4842-8300-4_7

An adversary with time, resources, and motivation will find a way into any network regardless of the size of the cybersecurity budget. This principle is entirely counter to the classic approach. Strategies that seem obvious under the lens of the classic approach now seem outdated and clearly flawed. Attempting to secure every element of your IT infrastructure to the same level doesn't make as much sense when you no longer believe it is possible to not get hacked. However, I would argue that this principle is more mature and results in a significantly more effective security program.

This principle is the foundation of the strategic defensive security approach and in this chapter, we will examine several different aspects of a well-built security program and contrast the classic approach with the strategic approach as our CISO is determining their approach to the sneaker company's cybersecurity.

Architecture

Just like any New York skyscraper, a strong cybersecurity program begins with the architecture. The architects are responsible for designing how the system will be laid out, the broad strokes of the implementation on a technical level, and the phases of capability construction. Architecture is where the priorities of the CISO become clear both in terms of technology and budget share as each are divvied up across the organization's IT landscape.

The Classic Approach

A CISO using a classic approach to their architecture is going to have one primary, often unspoken, goal – don't get hacked. Once this golden principle is accepted, the next step for our sneaker company CISO is to set the priorities for the various aspects of the IT footprint in terms of budget shares. While there are any number of ways to break down these decisions, the simplest approach is to view the business network in terms of internal and external. The internal network is considered to be the more sensitive side of the network. It is where internal processes are executed and generally is not accessible via the Internet without some form of authentication that hopefully prevents unauthorized access. The external network faces the Internet and provides the public with access to whatever applications, store fronts, etc. that are necessary to support the public offering of the company.

If our CISO's goal is to prevent any attack from becoming a full-blown compromise, then securing externally facing assets seems like the best place to start. Our CISO therefore prioritizes any assets that can be reached by a threat originating somewhere out there in the Internet. Our CISO reasons that these assets will be expected to weather the majority of attacks, they need to be the most secure resources within the organization. They are viewed as the wall the attacker must climb to get a glimpse of the more sensitive internal network.

Internal assets are not as high of a priority since the CISO, and his team of architects do not expect them to face as many threats. That is not to say that they are entirely neglected. The internal network will be secured as far as its lesser-prioritized budget will allow. For example, our CISO could obligate $2 million of the available $5 million for internal security, granting the larger share to the external side.

The classic approach results in a cybersecurity construct that very much resembles a medieval castle. The walls are large and thick. The defenders of the castle are perched on top of the walls waiting to shoot down any approaching attackers. Any attacker approaching the castle along the expected routes will find themselves intimidated by the defenses they are attempting to overcome. However, if one was able to view the castle from above, the security begins to show some weaknesses. Yes, the walls are big and strong but anyone who breaches them will find that there are few if any defenders within.

This classic approach has its flaws and from this overhead view, you may be already spotting them. If you've worked within the cybersecurity field for a few years, you may find this example contrived, overly simplistic, and yet...familiar. Don't blame our poor CISO. We can follow the logic; the path that leads from the core principle of "don't get hacked" to the emphasis on external asset protection to the consequential de-prioritization of the internal network and subsequent trust.

This approach is the reality for many companies of every size. During my experience on the offensive security side of the spectrum, my teams have referred to these networks as the "gooey center." All an attacker has to do is crack or get around that strong external shell and the internal network becomes a free-for-all. The security of the external assets will raise the bar for the skill required to compromise the network which, of course, will reduce the total number of compromises. However, when a compromise does occur, it has a much higher likelihood of being catastrophic.

The Strategic Approach

Our sneaker company CISO has been around the block a few times. He's seen the kind of security programs that are built on the golden principle and he isn't a fan. He opts to do away with the golden principle and instead starts with a different principle – "we will be hacked." Like we saw in the classical approach, the logic of prioritization will most often follow a natural path that originates and is based upon the guiding principle. But this time the guiding principle is different, and it will result in a different logical flow.

Our CISO calls a meeting with his team of security architects. He writes on the board, "We Will Be Hacked" before taking his seat. "I want to build our security program with the expectation that we will be compromised. Our goal is not to prevent every compromise, our goal is to develop architecture that will withstand a compromise without allowing a disruption to critical business operations. We will be compromise-resilient and we will render compromises inconsequential even though they will occur."

The ideas seem radical, but the team gets to work developing and then attempting to answer the questions that logically flow from this principle. What does this kind of network look like? How can network and security architecture be used to ensure continued business operations during a compromise?

Through the next few days and perhaps weeks, our CISO works with his architects. First, they determine that in order to ensure continued business operations, they must protect assets that are critical to those operations. That might include the primary public facing ecommerce site where their customers go to buy their sneakers. It might include the databases that hold sensitive client payment information for recurring purchases (only for the most dedicated sneaker-head). It might include the backend processing systems that allow credit card processing to occur. The team realizes that if they are to use the guiding principle of expecting a compromise, they must begin by prioritizing assets by their ability to affect critical business goals.

A layout begins to take form. A layout that looks like an unfinished connect-the-dots puzzle, wherein the dots represent network nodes considered critical to business goals. During this process, one architect examines the layout and speaks up. "Wait a minute. Where is the internal and external boundary line? How will we know which nodes we need to protect more if we don't know whether they are publicly or privately available?" The other architects examine the layout and consider the question. They realize that while in practice, defending public and private nodes will be different since they will not experience the same type of attacks, from a prioritization point of view, there is no difference. Technology and budget-share prioritization will be given to these critical nodes regardless of which side of the network they fall on.

The team quickly realizes that simply identifying critical nodes is not enough. The dots are not isolated. There are network paths and other hosts that connect them and, if compromised, these connections could also threaten business operations. However, these connections are not quite as critically important as the critical assets themselves. The team determines that the hosts directly connected to critical assets should be labeled as High in the criticality scale.

The team continues this process. The logical layout of network security is constructed like ripples in water. Critical assets are at the center with assets of lower criticality levels encircling them and expanding the further away from the critical asset they are.

A full week into the development of the architecture, a senior architect notices something and raises her hand. "There's too many connections. Half our network is rated at High criticality. We can't focus budget share and effort on half the network!" The other architects examine the designs and are forced to agree. Proximity to critical assets is everywhere. Afterall, as critical assets, they hold data that is going to be used by much of the network. The architect has an idea, "We need to reduce the connections; isolate the critical assets as much as possible. We'll need to construct connections to these critical assets with very tightly defined access and focus much of our defensive capabilities on those connections. That way, we will prioritize the critical asset as Critical, the connections as High, and the assets using the connections as Medium or perhaps even Low, depending on their ability to access levels of sensitive data."

After weeks of hard work, the team emerges exhausted and holding a plan that does not prioritize one large section of the network over the other. In fact, internal vs. external conversations were avoided entirely. The final plan contains a chain of assets that make up the most critical infrastructure for the continued operation and stability of the sneaker company. These assets will be prioritized over all others so that in case a compromise does occur, the core business assets will weather the storm.

These critical assets include the primary ecommerce website of the sneaker company, supporting databases with sensitive client data within the internal network, credit card processing servers, sneaker design and other intellectual property storage, and more.

The critical assets are prioritized regardless of their place in the network since a compromise of any asset in this chain would have a critical effect on the company objectives. The critical chain receives the necessary portion of the budget to ensure the architects are able to lock it down at a level commensurate with its priority. The next priority of assets is those that can affect business operations at a High rather than Critical level or those that have close access to critical assets and could be used to break into the critical chain. Outside of High are the Medium level assets and so on, with each level of assets receiving less budgeting and manpower prioritization.

The architects set about securing critical assets first, keeping in mind that assets that are not members of this chain have an expected higher chance of compromise. However, a compromise of these assets would have a less significant impact on core business objectives than the assets deemed critical.

Monitor and Detect

Both versions of our sneaker company CISO have completed their architectural plans. The classic version has a standard network focused on external security and a "don't get hacked" mentality, while the strategic version has a network focused on the security of what matters to company operations and a "we will get hacked" mentality.

Both versions now turn their attention to the next part of their security program – security monitoring and detection.

The Classic Approach

Our classic approach CISO begins constructing his security monitoring and threat detection program based upon the golden principle. Again, this principle is never really spoken. All members of the security team implicitly know that their mission is to simply not get hacked. Monitoring and detection capabilities will be focused onto that idea from the ground up.

As our CISO sets to work, they quickly discover a new principle as a logical result of the golden principle applied to monitoring and detection: Visibility is king! All IT assets must be monitored regardless of their location. Internal, external, cloud-based, or the break room smart fridge, everything must be monitored. Logs must be aggregated from every potential source so that detections that sweep across the entire network can be written. The core idea being that if you can't see it, you can't tell if it's under attack or gasp compromised! A network must eliminate blind spots to eliminate the threats lurking therein.

Our CISO performs research on the topic and finds himself in good company. Cybersecurity leaders reinforce his idea of the importance of visibility across the network. White papers have been written pushing the theory and building upon it.

With confidence in his approach, the CISO builds a list of the latest security features and solutions that he believes will best defend his network. He researches additional add-ons for solutions that will help automate the response to detected malicious activity. Finally, he begins the real-world implementation of the program by reaching out to the security solution vendors.

It is at this point that we spot the flaw in the classic approach. It is an item that all security programs grapple with, nearly all security professionals complain about, and the core reason that we can't make things as secure as we want to – Budget.

The CISO begins to review the cost of his approach and finds that the dominating pricing model for all aspects of his security monitoring and detection program is that they scale with size. The larger the network, the more they cost. Logging and aggregation solutions cost more as they process more data. Endpoint protection and monitoring cost more as more endpoints are protected. The add-ons to the given solutions that the CISO felt would greatly increase the network's resilience to attack add additional expenses, and once again, these expenses scale.

The CISO finds that he is forced to reevaluate his list. He trims down some of the more expensive plugins and selects less costly log aggregation solutions. He simply cannot afford to deploy the level of security solutions he would like in his network due to its size and must make compromises somewhere in order to achieve visibility across his network.

Our CISO ends the construction of his monitoring and detection program feeling rather depressed about the fact that budgets limited his ability to implement his golden principle. In the back of his mind, he realizes that by requiring every aspect of his network to have the same level of protection, while also being unable to pay for the level of protection he would have liked, his entire network is now less secure than he would have liked.

The Strategic Approach

Our classic CISO had lofty goals rooted in the best ideas for secure security program. It could be summarized as the philosophy of log, monitor, and detect everything. Unfortunately, it could not stand the reality of budget limitations and the very real-world effect they have on such goals.

The CISO using the strategic approach already has a vehicle to enable budget limitation considerations. That vehicle is the prioritization of assets with the network that was established during the creation of network security architecture. The philosophy of the strategic approach to security monitoring and detection could be summarized as log, monitor, and detect what matters.

The CISO goes through the same basic process that the classic approach CISO undertook. He begins by developing a list of security solutions that will best secure his network. It's an expensive list of some of the leading products complete with cutting-edge upgrades and add-ons. It's a list that would eat through his budget in a heartbeat if applied to the entire network. The CISO writes the world "Critical" across the top of that list and then sets it aside. He begins to write a second list. This list contains technologies that are slightly less featureful but still powerful. As you might guess, he writes the word "High" across the top of that list. A list is developed for every criticality level with decreasing features and a corresponding decrease in cost.

With these designs, the engineers set to work implementing the various levels of monitoring and detection products across the levels of criticality. Since the CISO has taken budget limitations into consideration at every level, he is not surprised by the final product. When the dust clears, the CISO finds that he has incredible capabilities allowing his team to protect the most critical assets.

Our CISO is well aware that this approach means that aspects of his network will be more "in the dark" than others. There will be places where a compromise could occur and not be immediately detected. However, his focus is on maintaining the strategic goals of the sneaker company. He is enabling the continued operations of critical business goals even in the face of a compromise. He is focused on ensuring that compromises, when they do occur, are not able to breach the upper echelons of network criticality.

I recognize that the ideas in this approach are controversial. Egalitarian visibility and monitoring are the core of modern security architecture. In theory, I entirely agree with this concept. If budgets were not a concern, then more data is always a good thing. Unfortunately, budgets are a concern, in fact, they are the primary limiting factor. Networks are not equal. Certain assets have a far greater ability to affect the overall mission of the organization than others. Ignoring this fact results in a network made less secure due to the ratio of its size against its budget. By securing everything to the same level, we lower the level to which everything is secure.

Investigate

Cyber investigation, more commonly called "hunting," is the process of proactively examining data within a given network for evidence of a compromise. It is an evolved approach that recognizes the shortcomings of standard reactive SOCs who are only aware of a compromise if an alert has been written for the actions that the attacker has taken. Threats evolve and organizations have to find ways of responding to new attacks and new types of compromise. Cyber investigation is a step in that direction.

Both versions of our CISO, the classic and the strategic, see value in the proactive approach of investigation and set out to develop the goals and guidelines of an investigation program.

The Classic Approach

Our golden principle-minded CISO isn't feeling the best after budget limitations derailed some of his goals for his monitoring program, but he discovers he still has some money left over for an investigation program. He is excited. He has heard so much about the developments in cyber hunting and threat intelligence and he can't wait to implement some of these new ideas in his environment.

He begins to build his team based on the same approach that many of his peers are using. Like much of cybersecurity, cyber investigation has largely been developed into a generalized "one size fits all" approach. Investigators (or "hunters") examine threat intelligence streams to learn trends in current threats and develop automated means of examining logs for those behaviors. Well-known behaviors of documented threats are recorded in standardized frameworks like the MITRE ATT&CK framework and investigators rely on them to hunt for behaviors of known threats. Threat intel streams and frameworks are often broken into broad categories of sectors such as federal, local, commercial, non-profit, financial, etc.

Our classic CISO instructs his team of investigators to ensure that all known actor techniques are easily detected by the monitoring capabilities. Threat streams are purchased and watched so that investigators know what new threats are occurring in the market in general and can ensure that the known behaviors for those sectors are detected.

The generalized approach may seem great for those that subscribe to the "don't get hacked" philosophy. After all, what harm could come from protecting yourself from the behaviors of all types of threats, even if they don't always apply to your industry? Organizations using this approach purchase membership to several threat intel streams and ensure that they are capable of detecting behaviors documented in hunting frameworks, assured that they are at least as aware of threats as other similar organizations.

The issue in this approach comes from the generality that exists at its core. Smaller organizations can use a generalized approach because they are at much less risk of being directly targeted. It is less likely that a somewhat sophisticated actor is developing target attacks against them. However, as an organization grows, the generalized approach to investigate becomes an ever-expanding blind spot. This blind spot exists in two ways. First, the organization is not aware and not prioritizing the specific attacks that are targeting them due to their "don't get hacked" approach, and second, the organization is not aware of the value a threat places on compromising their networks. This second concept takes a bit of unwrapping, so we'll examine it in detail in the next section.

The Strategic Approach

Like the classic CISO, the strategic CISO is also excited about cyber investigations and threat hunting. The difference between the two again comes down to the difference in their founding principles. Where the classic CISO used a general approach to his investigation program, the strategic CISO is interested in focusing his investigation on the specific threats that his organization faces.

Before he gets too deep into investigations, our strategic CISO wants to first determine the value of the assets he is trying to protect. That might seem pretty straightforward. If the CISO wants to protect the intellectual property for a sneaker that is currently being designed, for example, the value could be easily derived by determining how much revenue would be lost if the design were to be tampered with or leaked. The CISO could logically conclude that he should not spend a portion of the security budget protecting the shoe design that is greater than the amount of revenue that would be lost if the design were compromised.

There is a significant assumption at the core of this approach to valuation. This assumption represents a flaw in both the valuation process and the classic approach to threat investigation. The assumption is that the threat will value an organization's assets in the same way the organization does. From a security perspective, an asset's value is not solely determined by what an organization stands to gain from the asset. It is also determined by the attacker.

Let's take a break from the world of sneakers to explore this a bit further through a real-world scenario that I experienced during my career. I was performing security assessments and penetration tests for a Fortune 100 company. This company developed many widely used applications and the budget that was set aside to defend these applications was built on a given application's worth to the company. However, the company begins to encounter incredibly sophisticated attacks beyond the capabilities of the budget they had provided. They determined that foreign governments had a deep interest in attacking the company. At first, the company was confused. They were just a commercial company developing products like any other software company. Why would they be the target of a sophisticated nation state adversary? The answer was that the products the company developed were more valuable to the nation state adversary than they were to the company. The nation state wanted to obtain source code for those products to identify vulnerabilities since the US government widely used the products. The company was not aware of the kind of threats they faced. They used the same threat intel streams as others in the same market. They used the same generalized approach instead of working to understand the specific threats that they faced. They used their own valuation of their products and allowed that to drive their defense instead of determining how much their product was worth to an adversary.

General knowledge about the cyber threat landscape is very helpful, but it isn't the whole picture. An organization needs to identify the specific threats it is facing and understand the level of resources that threat is willing to spend compromising the organization. As an organization grows, general threat and adversary technique knowledge becomes less and less useful since threats have an increasingly varied set of reasons for attacking it.

Getting back to our CISO, he believes that his organization is large enough that an examination of more specific threats is in order. His team of investigators returns after sometime to inform him that the sneaker designs are actually quite novel in the market place and have a chance to revolutionize a section of the market. Competitors are very interested in the intellectual property and may even be attempting various forms of corporate espionage to obtain the designs. The CISO realizes that protecting the shoe designs will require more of a budget than he had originally considered through his revenue-based valuation.

Frameworks

If you've worked in cybersecurity or managed virtually any application that was used by the federal government, the military, processed credit cards, or something else considered sensitive, you've undoubtably encountered certification frameworks. These frameworks are created by large government, military, or commercial entities to ensure that a product, application, network, etc. meets a minimum security standard. If you've worked with credit card processing applications, then you've had to deal with PCI certification. If you've attempted to sell cloud-based applications to the US federal government, you've encountered FedRAMP. The FedRAMP process is illustrated in Figure 7-1.

Figure 7-1. *FedRAMP Authorization Process*

Certification frameworks are an important part of ensuring a standard level of security before an application is trusted with some level of sensitive information. Unfortunately, these frameworks do little to ensure the resilience of the applications and networks they are applied to.

We will take the example of the Federal Risk and Authorization Management Program, more commonly called FedRAMP. FedRAMP is a certification framework specifically applied to cloud-based offerings and is used to ensure a level of security among these offerings as they are sold to the United States federal government. FedRAMP is one of the most modern certification frameworks. In my opinion, it does a pretty good job. Its requirements are more in-depth than most frameworks and more aware of the intricacies of the various cybersecurity disciplines they span.

For all the forward thinking of the FedRAMP requirements, it is still based on that golden principle of the classic approach – don't get hacked. It has no requirements regarding the resiliency of the application nor any requirements that dictate how data exposure could be minimized to help render compromises inconsequential. Like most of the cybersecurity industry, the FedRAMP framework does not consider that a portion of the application that attains its certification will inevitably be compromised at some point.

When we examine FedRAMP in the context of expecting a compromise regardless of how good the standards are, the blind-spot of resiliency becomes obvious. If security is only half the battle, FedRAMP is only half a framework.

We can apply this context to practically every other certification framework that is similar to FedRAMP. The Risk Management Framework (RMF) was originally created in 2004 by NIST and then updated in 2018 through NIST SP 800-37. This framework is used by every agency of the US federal government and the DoD. It defines a high-level seven-step process for securing systems through an Authorization to Operate (ATO) and ongoing risk management, often referred to as continuous monitoring. The intent of RMF is to be technology agnostic so that it can be used to apply security and risk management at every level.

You can problem-guess what's coming. RMF is built on the golden principle and lives in a world where compromises do not happen if security controls are tight. Its seven steps can be summarized as

1. Prepare

2. Categorize information systems

3. Select security controls

4. Implement security controls

5. Assess security controls

6. Authorize information system

7. Monitor security controls

Figure 7-2 illustrates these steps in a commonly shown depiction of the RMF process presented by NIST and other organizations that implement it.

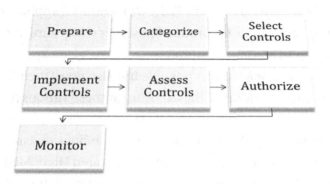

Figure 7-2. *RMF Steps*

What's missing here? Perhaps an eighth step called "Simulate security control failure," and a ninth step called "Minimize compromise impact"? Again, if we come from the understanding that a portion of the systems secured through RMF will still be compromised, then suddenly the steps as they are established by NIST seem like an unfinished sentence.

I won't bore you by examining every certification framework. Rest assured that CNMC, PCI, and others suffer from the same lack of resiliency consideration. They are frameworks that are missing half the battle.

So what would a framework that considers both security and resiliency look like? We are already beginning to see some movement in that direction within the industry. These movements have been spurred on by the rise in ransomware attacks. The term "ransomware attack" is interesting. Ransomware is not an attack. Ransomware is a payload executed after a successful attack. This differentiation is important because it shows that ransomware is only highlighting the compromises that were already occurring. Our applications were already compromised, our frameworks were already failing. Ransomware just turned up the stakes.

143

Let's return to the FedRAMP discussion. How could FedRAMP be changed to consider the importance of resiliency and compromise survivability? Again, we begin with the idea that a compromise will occur. If we accept that fact, then the next step is to gain an understanding of the consequences of compromise at different levels. In addition to its enforcement of security standards, FedRAMP-certified applications should provide an impact analysis for production server compromise, database compromise, cloud account compromise, etc. The given applications should attempt to be as secure as possible but also grant their federal customers an understanding of the exposure at these various levels of compromise.

In the current FedRAMP framework, vulnerabilities that are identified through the assessment of security controls are rated High, Medium, or Low severity and given time windows for remediation. If the vulnerability cannot be remediated due to the functionality's importance to the overall product, the certifying federal agency must either accept the risk or reject the product. This concept could be applied to the resiliency side of the framework. The application seeking certification would provide data on the exposure that results from various compromise scenarios. If the exposure is unacceptable, the company selling the application must work to minimize the exposure and increase the resiliency of its product.

FedRAMP is a convenient example, but the focus on resiliency as an equally important objective as security can be woven into any cybersecurity framework.

Auditing

A framework is only as good as the standards of its audits. RMF, for example, was intended to be a flexible framework applied at any level without consideration for the specific technology it was applied against. However, in practice, RMF can become little more than a checklist. Its deeper implications and intentions can be lost when auditing practices are not firm, documented, and enforced.

Auditing within a framework that implements resiliency would require the simulation of compromise scenarios and then examination of what data or impact those compromises can affect. FedRAMP already requires an in-depth review of all security controls and their implementation and even establishes thorough requirements for a penetration test. If FedRAMP were to be expanded to consider resiliency then a resiliency test, similar to a penetration test, would be included. Different levels of compromise would be created within the application seeking certification and the auditors would examine what data is exposed. Risk ratings would be applied to the exposure and the company developing the application would be required to implement better resiliency policies to reduce the risk ratings and obtain certification.

Theoretical Case Studies

So far, we've explored the concepts of strategic defensive security within the context of commercial companies almost exclusively. In the next section, I'd like to demonstrate how the same concepts can be applied to other sectors through the use of hypothetical case studies.

The Architecture of Accountable Sectors

The Springfield Children's hospital has discovered that it is the victim of a ransomware attack. Five doctors are unable to access their data and treat their patients. The ransomware demands a payment in crypto currency. After a brief meeting, the hospital directors pay the ransom and re-gain control of the computers.

This experience has shaken the trust that the directors have in their IT infrastructure. They call in their director of network security and ask how they can be sure that these kinds of attacks will never be successful again. The director simply states that they cannot be sure. In fact, similar attacks will most likely be successful in the future. The hospital directors task the director of network security with re-architecting the security program and, if necessary, the network itself to account for these kinds of attacks and to protect that which is most important to the hospital. The director of network security gets to work.

The director recently read a book on Strategic Defensive Security and decides to use that approach. The first step he takes is to define the mission objectives of the security of the hospital. From his research, he defines three such objectives and ranks them in order:

1. Protect patient lives

2. Protect patient health data

3. Ensure continued hospital operations

The next step is to identify the network nodes that have the ability to affect these objectives and assign the nodes a criticality level. The director examines network diagrams and identifies the systems directly responsible for the control of life support systems and marks them with a critical severity. Next, he notes any node which has the ability to affect life support nodes and marks them at a high severity. He continues through several rounds of increasing distance from life support nodes and corresponding decreases in criticality rating.

With network nodes associated with the first objective prioritized, the director moves on to nodes that hold sensitive patient health data. Through the same process, all nodes that have some proximity or ability to affect patient health data are prioritized. And finally, the process is repeated for the third objective.

The director pauses a moment and realizes that there are hundreds of network nodes capable of affecting these three objectives in some way or that are close enough within the network to affect nodes that could affect the objectives. He sets to work re-architecting the network with the goal of reducing the number of nodes with higher criticality rankings. He uses subnets, firewalls, and more to lock the most critical nodes off from the rest of the network except for defined access points. For networks relating to life support, the director splits them to their own network entirely with no connection to the general hospital network or the Internet.

With the number of nodes that need higher levels of protection reduced to the bare minimum, the director commissions his threat intelligence experts to create a profile of the kinds of threats the network will face. Their goal is to determine the level of value that threats place on hospital network. With this profile, the director will be aware of what parts of his network are valued higher by threat actors than the value the hospital itself might assign.

The security director examines his budget and selects cybersecurity products across a range of categories. Log aggregation, endpoint protection, etc. He implements the products with the greatest feature set on the most critical components and directs his Security Operations Center to prioritize events on those nodes above all others. Nodes with lower criticality ratings are assigned products with reduced cost as well as feature sets.

With the architecture and monitoring aspects of the network established, the director focuses on increasing the resiliency of the network to a compromise.

Military Resiliency

We've talked a little about resiliency and how necessary it is within the commercial sector. Within military sectors, it's a core requirement. Of course, the military isn't new to the concept of resiliency. Wars are messy and combat in any form is disruptive and unpredictable by nature. So how does the military foster resiliency before engaging with an enemy? Training and experience are important factors but perhaps the most well-known test of resiliency outside of warfare is war games.

War games are a simulation of a battle. Both sides are staffed by military members attempting to outmaneuver the other. Creativity is encouraged and unexpected scenarios are guaranteed to occur. These games help commanders understand how to react when aspects of the infrastructure they rely upon are less than ideal or outright fail. But war games are used at every level. For example, the last step in the US Navy Boot Camp is a simulation called Battle Stations. During the 12-hour exercise, sailor candidates use their training to perform the mundane maintenance of a ship, while also responding to a number of catastrophic scenarios.

This style of building and evaluating resiliency is very similar to some of the ideas used within cybersecurity. Earlier we mentioned the Chaos Monkey project by Netflix which enforces resiliency by randomly shutting down servers within the Netflix production environment. Both of these approaches ensure resilience by creating unstable environments.

So how can we apply these concepts to military IT systems to foster and enforce resiliency at the level required by military objectives? If you have some experience within the cybersecurity community, you may be thinking that I'm about to discuss the common simulations that exist within the cybersecurity community today. These simulations are almost always Capture the Flag competitions, with defenders set on one side and attackers on the other. One well-known example of these CTF challenges is the National Collegiate Cyber Defense Competition wherein colleges compete to defend their simulated networks against trained penetration testers. These types of challenges are fun and have their place in cybersecurity education, but they are far from realistic. Cyber dogfighting across networks in real time is not a reality. CTFs should not be considered a viable means of learning resiliency.

Let's create a hypothetical case study. The military of Australia has realized that their IT networks were built with the outdated idea of "don't get hacked." Networks built with this principal are not resilient. They are built to prevent a compromise with the naive expectation that such a thing is possible.

Upon review, the Australian military leaders realize that they face advanced threats from around the world and compromise is inevitable. In fact, their systems are most likely already compromised to some level by the most advanced toolkits in the world. In addition, they are concerned that ransomware attacks and other debilitating threats could decrease the nation's preparedness for responding to a military threat.

The Australians decide to re-architect their cybersecurity program and part of that process is taking steps to create resilience within their IT networks so that a compromise is not able to significantly affect the military readiness. To accomplish this, they create cyber war game scenarios. The scenarios for these games include ransomware randomly deployed to a user's box, a domain controller compromised, an entire base losing Internet access, and more. These scenarios are executed as tabletop exercises at first, then they are conducted within test environments that mimic real military networks. But the Australian military leaders know that resilience is not achieved until the actual networks that are relied upon are put under the stress of cyberattack.

The Australian cyber command begins conducting simulated cyberattacks within the networks of various bases. The base commanders are given a warning that some level of attack will occur within a given window and a variety of compromise scenarios will be executed. In response to these cyber war games, new creative approaches are developed to maintain military IT objectives even during a significant compromise. Secondary fail-over networks are developed, sensitive data is available in fewer areas, and workstations are virtualized so that a response to a compromise can occur more quickly.

CHAPTER 8

Infinite Cybersecurity

Infinite cybersecurity, what a term. It certainly sounds like some of the other buzzword soup that has become so commonplace in the industry, doesn't it? I suspect if the concept was viewed as valid then, just like with any other concept, vendors would start stretching the definition to apply to products or services they already know how to offer until it falls into cyber purgatory just like cloud, cyber kill chain, blockchain, machine learning, and others.

The cybersecurity industry and its customers face an infinite number of adversaries that are infinitely varied in their sophistications and motivations, and we have been doing so with a decidedly finite mindset. Much of the first portion of this book covered how the finite mindset has impacted the industry and how vendors advertise their capabilities even though the term finite was not directly called out. When we use terms like "stop threats," "prevent data leaks," "secure your environment," and "block ransomware," we are embracing the finite mindset.

The Infinite Game

Simon Sinek is a British-American author and public speaker who wrote a book and has given countless talks, including TED Talks, on the concept of the infinite game, which is a similar take in ideas to James P. Carse's work *Finite and Infinite Games*. Full credit to Simon for bringing the concept into public light and conveying it in such a way that it can be applied to almost any situation. Essentially, the concept is that there are finite games and infinite games.

© Dr. Jacob G. Oakley, Michael Butler, Wayne York, Dr. Matthew Puckett, Dr. J. Louis Sewell 2022
J. G. Oakley et al., *Theoretical Cybersecurity*, https://doi.org/10.1007/978-1-4842-8300-4_8

A finite game is one where there are known players on known teams playing by established rules with a specific win condition. In such finite games the players are playing to win the game, think a sports game, or chess. Infinite games are those with known and unknown players on known and unknown teams who can join, leave, or return at any time and where the rules are always changeable. Infinite games do not necessarily have a start or a beginning and the players are not playing to win, they are playing to stay in the game, think business or an insurgency.

The Lesson

As applied to business, warfare, and other areas, the most important aspect of finite and infinite games is that the players know what type of game they are in so they can play to the appropriate motivation. If we look at one of Simon's examples, in the Vietnam War, the United States was playing a finite strategy, trying to "win," whereas the local opposition was trying to simply stay in the game long enough for the US to drop out. Similarly, this played out recently and to successful conclusion by the opposition playing the right game and the US playing the wrong game in Afghanistan as well. The US was trying to "win" in Afghanistan, where the Taliban was simply trying to stay in the game until the US dropped out. When a player does not know the type of game they are actually playing, they cannot optimize play or hope to improve their position.

Infinite Cybersecurity

The crux of the finite and infinite game concept in application to cybersecurity is that cybersecurity is an infinite game. New threat actors can target a defender at any time, some may give up targeting a vendor at any time. The attackers do not play by any rules and the goal of the defenders should be to keep playing (operating their business or organization in the face of threats). Instead, as we have already covered to some degree, the cybersecurity industry talks a lot like American generals and politicians did regarding the conflicts in Vietnam and Afghanistan.

Theoretical cybersecurity efforts should be aimed at moving the body of work and industry as a whole toward using the infinite game mindset so that we can best address, mitigate, and coexist with the threats on the playing field. Exploration of new cybersecurity paradigms that make us and our customers better players in an infinite game should result in more relevant and effective solutions, capabilities, and services that will look less like sunk costs and more like strategic enablers.

Weaknesses and a Strength

Accepting that cybersecurity is an infinite game where innumerous threats are playing without rules against the defenders our industry supports, we must identify the strengths and weaknesses of our customers and their opponents. For the sake of keeping this discussion to a single chapter, we will primarily focus on three areas where attackers or defenders might have a unique advantage or disadvantage.

Time

Time is a strength for the attacker and not the defender. Some attackers will be unsophisticated, only have a passing interest or even be automated. However, since some may also be nation-state actors, we must assume that the collective adversary, to include any possible attacker, has the ability to spend essentially infinite time trying to compromise a defending network. Conversely, the defender only has a set amount of personnel who can work only a set number of hours in the configuration, maintenance, and defense of the organization. Advantage attackers.

Money

Money, or more broadly resources in general, are also a strength for the attacker and not defender. Since we have assumed all potential threats to include APTs and nation-states, we realize that if the target is important enough, resources and expenditures can essentially be considered infinite. Where national security is concerned, it should not be surprising the great lengths some governments will go to protect it. Just as with time, the defenders are limited by things like budgets and emergency funds and as such will only be able to spend a finite amount of money or resources on protection over any given period. Advantage attackers.

Information and Access

The imbalance of money and time regarding nation-state level threats and APTs compared to their targets is a somewhat conveyed and understood concept, especially in cybersecurity circles. What is less explored and rarely capitalized is the distinct benefit defenders have from their access to and information of their own attack surface, systems, and organization. Attackers are spending time and money to gain information and ultimately access to what the defenders already have. In an infinite game, as players with a unique advantage, defenders need to leverage this as infinite players in the most complete and continuous way possible.

Finite Battles in an Infinite War

Some adversaries will set themselves up for finite, win or lose battles in the larger infinite war. This is where cost benefit comes into play. Actors that are financially motivated (APTs, organized crime) are likely to set some bounds on their activity because at a point, their time and money no longer provide a cost benefit based on a given target. For example, in our Transexperiafax target anecdote from previous chapters, an attacker has

154

some very specific metrics they could use to determine the profitability of such a target and leverage that information to bound finite game durations, incorporating profitability as an activity limiter. If profitability starts to diminish due to a shrinking cost benefit, the adversary can simply drop out of the game against that specific defender and move on to another more profitable target.

Defenders can do this too, both by manufacturing finite battles as well or recognizing where finite battles will occur with their organization in a greater infinite conflict. Take, for example, a company that operates a global small-satellite constellation in low earth orbit (LEO). Let's say the company provides imaging services. Now, the organization itself wants to play the infinite game. Strategically, it wants to continue to operate the satellites and sell imaging services as long as possible. As such, cybersecurity too must be played broadly in an infinite sense by infinite-minded players.

There are aspects of the attack surface, however, that lend themselves to more finite perspectives and can be fought on finite grounds. The operation of the organization may be hopefully unbounded by time, but the lifespan of LEO satellites is decidedly not. They may be operationally capable for only a matter of two or three years. That operational can be leveraged to bound the cybersecurity effort on that portion of the attack surface represented by the system of systems of systems that is a satellite constellation. The defenders can now make cybersecurity and risk decisions that are in a somewhat bounded environment, limited by operational durations. This means that risk mitigation and cost benefit are considerations for a specific timeline and can be tailored toward winning a defined two-to-three-year battle, instead of an endless one.

This example is arguably a gross oversimplification, but I think it does well to highlight that there are certainly aspects of an organization's strategic operations that can be taken as winnable finite games in the larger accepted infinite game construct that must be acknowledged.

Applying the Theory

Applying infinite game theory to cybersecurity implementations is and will not be an easy concept. Cybersecurity struggles to find justification or prove capability where there are no easy metrics of success. Unfortunately, those are precisely the areas where cybersecurity is needed most. We will discuss a few high-level applications that look to improve infinite cybersecurity game play and use graphical diagrams to illustrate how they and other principles can help improve any organization's chances at infinite participation.

The best way to apply this is to identify the cases where we can gain an advantage on as many attackers as possible, while intelligently ceding that there are some (nation-states) where there is no ceiling or timeline for us to shortcut. In those cases, we must simply attempt to close on their curve as much as possible.

Adversary as a Service (AaaS)

OK, so maybe that was a jab at the preponderance of [insert thing] as a service (*aaS) terms and capabilities being slung around willy-nilly. In all seriousness, this is a concept I have discussed at length with other cybersecurity professionals, and it seems to be focused on the infinite game as well as relying on the one advantage defenders do hold in that game, self-knowledge and access.

Typically, some of the most powerful defensive operations an organization can undertake are robust monitoring capabilities and threat-hunting campaigns. Unfortunately, monitoring, and to a greater degree threat hunting, rely on admittedly outdated and non-standardized intelligence to help them zero in on malicious activity in the network. Even frameworks like MITRE's ATT&CK are based on often aged, incomplete, and largely open source information. This means that hunting based on these facts is likely to find you someone re-using a capability, forgotten access, or tools or help you walk your way down a false flag operation. This is of course because the bad guys also have access to this framework, so they know how different actions, techniques, and tools are attributed.

What if, instead of heavily relying on threat intelligence, we created our own intelligence as an adversary such as a nation-state might? After all, we have access already, we know our own strategic outcomes and goals and how we are going about them. We know our own IT refresh cycles, upgrade and update schedules, etc. Why not create intelligence about our own organization like a nation-state might and leverage that kind of information to inform things like hunt and monitoring as well.

Performing this type of activity is a sort of pseudo red teaming that, when coupled with proactive assessments afforded by penetration testing and red teaming, can help an organization mitigate risk based on self-knowledge and largely agnostic of threat specificity. By not focusing on individual threats and instead focusing on self-knowledge, informed intelligence defenders might be able to force multiply their ability to combat larger groups of potential threats.

In a way, this is a next step to practices like resilience. With resilience, we take an understanding of ourselves and our needs to inform risk-reducing practices aimed at keeping an organization in the game. Having an organic adversary as a service capability allows us to red team our own resilience decision matrix and inform threat-hunting campaigns in a way that supports continued pursuit of strategic goals. Withstand as many threats as possible without trying to fight off specific threats.

Attacking the Curve

A former colleague of mine, contributing author Dr. Sewell, asked an interesting non-cyber question that really got me thinking about how to attack the curve (heavy graphical representation of the curve I am talking about soon to follow). He asked: "How long might it take an adversary to find and weaponize a vulnerability in something like routing infrastructure?"

I was not sure, but that was not the point, I said perhaps three to five years maybe. His next question was: "What if every three years, then, we just switch our routing infrastructure to a new brand entirely, such as from Cisco to Juniper, moving the target on the adversary?"

Now there is a lot to poke at, but broadly, this is a very interesting concept. We can't have a steeper or continuous curve like some nation-states might in targeting us (if we think our organization is actually the target of such efforts). However, maybe we can attack the adversary's efficiencies in the aspects of time and resources as they play an infinite game with us.

Before we go through the graphs to follow, I must assert that there is a distinct difference in how you approach attacking the curve when talking about criminal organizations and other lower tier APTs compared to nation-states. As we mentioned, the former has cost benefit in mind, the latter have national security in mind and their curve can be steep and unending if they feel it necessary. For nation-states, cost benefit in this sense is not really a consideration.

Cost Benefit Refined

In Chapter 3, we discussed cost benefit and how the adversary and the organization may have differing opinions on what cost beneficial cybersecurity or cyberattack spending looks like, which affects an organization's ability to adequately resource its protective strategies. Instead, later on here, we will show how adversaries like criminal organizations might approach their cost benefit line as it pertains to spending time and money before leaving the game if they have not gotten access or information necessary at that point. Figure 8-1 shows an adversary spending personnel hours over time to achieve compromise with a limiting cost benefit line. The adversary is going to spend a lot of hours up front trying to gain access and information, while later spending few hours to siphon out data. They will either abandon the attack if it looks unlikely to have cost benefit or be successful.

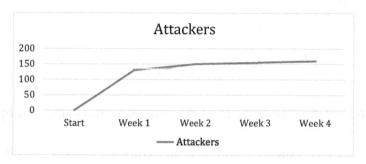

Figure 8-1. *Attacker Personnel Hours*

On the other hand, the defender will spend personnel hours in a predictable way, their cybersecurity person working forty-hour work weeks over the course of the month as shown in Figure 8-2.

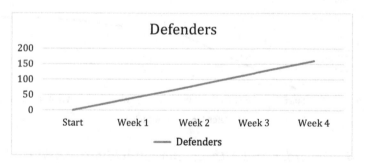

Figure 8-2. *Defender Personnel Hours*

Figure 8-3 shows the two alongside each other.

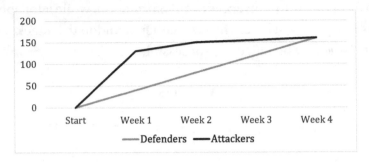

Figure 8-3. *Defender and Attacker personnel hours (limited to 160)*

It is important to accept that the more realistic scenario is probably that the adversary is willing to spend more than 160 hours in a month or have more than one person in the initial phases, which means it could also be as disparate as Figure 8-4, where the adversary has decided it can spend 400 personnel hours and still get a justifiable profit from the compromise.

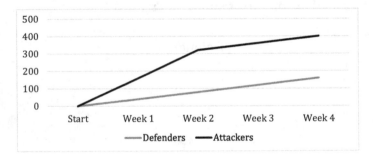

Figure 8-4. *Defender and Attacker personnel hours (realistic)*

Figure 8-5 is a different way of portraying Figure 8-3, and Figure 8-6 is a different way of showing Figure 8-4 to highlight the area of the surface between the two curves.

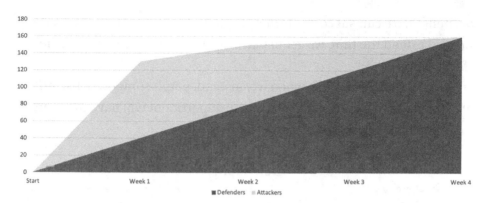

Figure 8-5. *Highlighted Defender and Attacker personnel hours (limited to 160)*

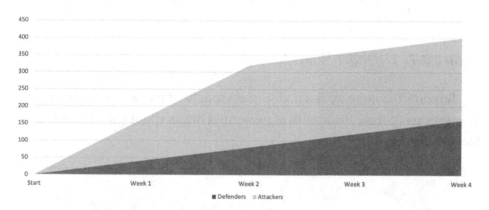

Figure 8-6. *Highlighted Defender and Attacker personnel hours (realistic)*

What Figures 8-5 and 8-6 do a good job of showing is the shaded region between the line graphs. This shaded area is essentially a mathematical representation of the disadvantage faced as a surface area. Anything a defender can do to decrease this surface area is a worthwhile approach to cybersecurity. In these examples, our adversary has a bounded finite battle in the greater infinite cybersecurity conflict. If we as defenders can increase the surface area or lower or move the defender's line of

161

cost benefit, we can successfully impact their ability to win a finite battle and also extend the time we get to play and that they have to play in the infinite game.

So what does it look like when we, instead, graph something like an APT? Well, our one-person cybersecurity department will have the same personnel hour graph, as shown in Figure 8-7.

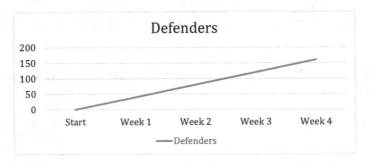

Figure 8-7. *Defender Hours Graph*

But now the attacker is a nation-state that feels its national security interests are at stake, its month of personnel hours spent will probably look like this Figure 8-8.

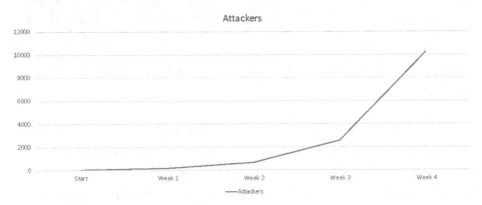

Figure 8-8. *Attacker Hours Graph*

The striking difference in effort and the advantage of the attacker regarding time is shown in Figure 8-9.

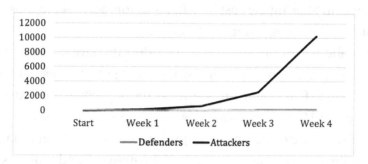

Figure 8-9. *Comparing Hours Spent*

Now when we shade in the surface area of disadvantage, we get a stark representation of the imbalance involved, as shown in Figure 8-10.

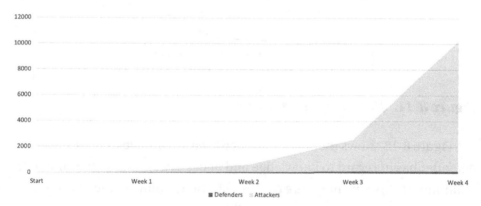

Figure 8-10. *Effort Gap as Surface Area*

Graphs for resources or expenditure would look much the same as the ones we have done with time, so I will not repeat them. These graphs represent a surface area of disadvantage that can be attacked by doing things to increase the defenders surface area, decrease the attackers surface area, or shorten the runway for the attacker to run out of cost benefit. All of this is typically only possible in a semi-bounded, finite conflict, where we hope hackers like criminal organizations essentially have a bottom line. The nation-state graph should show the relative hopelessness in altering the cost benefit equation because, to those organizations, there might not be a bottom line.

So how about the one area where defenders do have the advantage? Let's take a look at graphs representing knowledge and access. Figure 8-11 shows how the defender starts by knowing about 100% of the network and having access to 100% of the machines and the attacker starts at zero, but how, over the course of a month, compromises those numbers change. Ultimately, the attacker has access to half the network and ransoms it to the defenders.

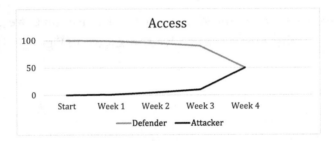

Figure 8-11. *Knowledge and Access*

Figure 8-12 shows the shaded surface area advantage that the defender has in regard to knowledge and access. Attempts at continuously maintaining this advantage are our best chance in playing the infinite cybersecurity game for as long as possible.

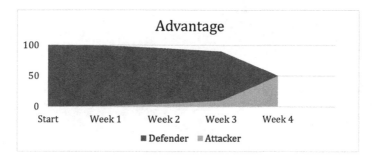

Figure 8-12. *Defender Advantage*

Summary

This chapter has identified that cybersecurity is not a finite game but an infinite one. This builds upon what we have already learned about preconceived notions, misconceptions, and misconstruing that happens in the cybersecurity industry. We can see that theoretical cybersecurity concepts like strategic cybersecurity, and now infinite cybersecurity, are the real path forward for the industry and the only way to effectively grow the body of work beyond sales pitches and profit margins. At a high level, we have discussed possible concepts that would involve performing and implementing more infinitely minded cybersecurity, but the real challenge is up to you the reader and the industry at large to embrace the theoretical and eventually practical pursuit of these sorts of concepts. Once again, resiliency has been called out as the naturally occurring evolution to participation in the infinite game, which further highlights the need for us to innovate in such directions rather than be pushed toward them, as has been the case. The following chapters, Chapter 9 and Chapter 10, are intended to represent what an academic pursuit of researching and proving out an example of this concept might look like. This is intended to foster further development of theoretical cybersecurity innovation.

CHAPTER 9

Cybersecurity and Game Theory

Game theory is the mathematical study of interactions between players. It has been applied extensively to social sciences such as economics. Cybersecurity has a social component in the sense that players can have co-operative or adversarial relationships. We will frame cybersecurity in terms of game theory. Note that many concepts elsewhere in the book can be analyzed using game theory.

We will begin with a contrived example to illustrate the benefit of modeling cybersecurity using game theory. This example is not realistic; it is only intended to illustrate a key difference between game theory models and other methods for analyzing cybersecurity problems. We will construct more realistic models in the next chapter.

For completeness, we will give a brief explanation of expected value. Intuitively, expected value is an average of possible payoffs weighted by probability. We use the term payoff in order to be consistent with game theory terminology. For example, the calculation of expected payoff from

Outcome	Probability	Payoff
A	0.1	20
B	0.2	-10
C	0.3	5
Other	0.4	0

Figure 9-1. *Expected Value Example*

© Dr. Jacob G. Oakley, Michael Butler, Wayne York, Dr. Matthew Puckett, Dr. J. Louis Sewell 2022
J. G. Oakley et al., *Theoretical Cybersecurity*, https://doi.org/10.1007/978-1-4842-8300-4_9

Figure 9-1 is the following: $EV = 0.1(20) + 0.2(-10) + 0.3(5) + 0.4(0)$. Note that expected value can be positive, negative, or zero. We will use the terms expected gain and expected loss to emphasize that expected value is positive or negative, respectively.

Our example game has two players, one attacker and one defender. The game occurs in two stages. In the first stage, the defender chooses how many units to spend on cybersecurity. In the second stage, the attacker chooses whether or not to attack. If the defender spent 0 units, the attack will be successful with probability 1. For each unit thereafter, the probability that the attack will be successful decreases by half. The attacker must spend 1 unit in order to attack. If the attack is successful, the attacker gains 10 units, and the defender loses 10 units. We will assume that the attacker will attack if the expected value of the attack is greater than the cost. In other words, the attacker will attack if $10p > 1$, where p is the probability that the attack is successful.

Suppose the defender tries to develop a strategy without considering the attacker's strategy. The defender reasons as follows. It is worthwhile to spend 1 unit on cybersecurity if it decreases the defender's expected loss from an attack by more than 1. Otherwise, it is not worthwhile. The calculations of the defender's expected net loss are summarized in Figure 9-2. The defender chooses to spend 3 units, and the probability of success of the attack is $p = \dfrac{1}{8}$. The attacker chooses to attack, since the expected gain from the attack is $\dfrac{1}{8} \cdot 10 = 1.25$, which is greater than the 1 unit spent to attack. The attacker's expected net payoff is $1.25 - 1 = 0.25$. The defender's expected net loss is $-3 - 1.25 = -4.25$. The expected loss consists of the 3 units spent on cybersecurity and the expected 1.25 loss from the cyberattack.

Suppose that the defender has complete information about the attacker. That information includes the attacker's payoffs and strategy. In that case, the defender can improve by utilizing game theory. The attacker will choose to attack if the probability of success is greater than $\dfrac{1}{10}$, since the expected gain from the attack is greater than 1 unit. Similarly, the attacker will choose not to attack if the probability of success is less than $\dfrac{1}{10}$. The calculations are summarized in Figure 9-3. The optimum strategy for the defender is to spend 4 units on cybersecurity. In that case, the attacker chooses not to attack and has a payoff of 0. The defender's expected loss is −4.

Units	Prob of Success	Expected Loss from Attack	Expected Net Loss
0	1	$1(-10) = -10$	0-10=-10
1	$\dfrac{1}{2}$	$\dfrac{1}{2}(-10) = -5$	-1-5=-6
2	$\dfrac{1}{4}$	$\dfrac{1}{4}(-10) = -2.5$	-2-2.5=-4.5
3	$\dfrac{1}{8}$	$\dfrac{1}{8}(-10) = -1.25$	-3-1.25=-4.25
4	$\dfrac{1}{16}$	$\dfrac{1}{16}(-10) = -0.625$	-4-0.625=-4.625
5	$\dfrac{1}{32}$	$\dfrac{1}{32}(-10) = -0.3125$	-5-0.3125=-5.3125

Figure 9-2. *Defender's Expected Loss Assuming Attack Occurs*

Without considering the attacker's strategy, the defender concluded that it was not worthwhile to spend the fourth unit on cybersecurity. The flaw in that reasoning was not considering that the defender can influence the attacker's behavior. The evolution of strategy is a key concept in modeling cybersecurity using game theory. Attackers are always adapting to defenders, and defenders are always adapting to attackers. Changing the strategy of key players can influence the entire game.

The remainder of the chapter presents elementary concepts of game theory in the context of cybersecurity. We will not assume any knowledge of advanced mathematics. Therefore, terms and concepts will be described using plain language. Our goal is to present game theory in a way that is intuitive to understand while still being consistent with a more rigorous approach.

Units	Prob of Success	Attack Occurs	Attacker's EV	Defender's EV
0	1	Yes	$10 - 1 = 9$	$0 - 10 = -10$
1	$\dfrac{1}{2}$	Yes	$5 - 1 = 4$	$-1 - 5 = -6$
2	$\dfrac{1}{4}$	Yes	$2.5 - 1 = 1.5$	$-2 - 2.5 = -4.5$
3	$\dfrac{1}{8}$	Yes	$1.25 - 1 = 0.25$	$-3 - 1.25 = -4.25$
4	$\dfrac{1}{16}$	No	0	-4
5	$\dfrac{1}{32}$	No	0	-5

Figure 9-3. *Attacker and Defender EV Assuming Optimal Attacker Strategy*

The Infinite Cybersecurity Game

Game theory models are usually constructed with many simplifying assumptions so that conclusive analysis can be done. Instead of incorporating simplifying assumptions immediately, we will begin by outlining how to construct a game theory model for cybersecurity as a whole. Previous work in this area has focused mainly on the interaction between an attacker and defender during a single cyberattack. We are concerned with attacker and defender strategies over time and how those strategies evolve.

For the purposes of this model, we will consider the cybersecurity game to be infinite. Technically, it is a finite game with unknown duration which ends when cybersecurity is no longer relevant. Many games have discrete stages, but events in the cybersecurity game occur in real time.

In the following sections, we will define key terms related to game theory. We will also describe the related elements of the cybersecurity game.

Players in the Cybersecurity Game

We place two requirements for an individual or organization to be considered a player in the cybersecurity game: the player must have the ability to protect or compromise cyber assets, and the player must experience gain or loss from doing so. The ability to protect or compromise cyber assets may be either direct or indirect. For example, an individual may discover and publicize software exploits, but not make use of them. The gain or loss may be financial or otherwise. For example, if an individual launches cyberattacks for fun, then fun is the gain.

We will define several categories of players in the cybersecurity game. Attackers attempt to directly compromise cyber assets in order to realize some gain. As discussed regarding the 1-9-90 principle in Chapter 3, the types and capabilities of attackers vary greatly. Attackers include nation-states, criminal organizations, and lone individuals. Defenders attempt to directly protect cyber assets in order to prevent losses. Defenders include government agencies, corporations, and individuals with personal computers.

Other types of players influence the cybersecurity game without directly interacting with cyber assets. Governments/law enforcement attempt to protect cyber assets by passing and enforcing laws. Cybersecurity providers attempt to protect cyber assets by providing hardware, software, and services. While cybersecurity providers experience gains and losses based on earnings, cybersecurity outcomes influence those earnings.

In many games, there is a concept of "nature." Essentially, nature is responsible for all actions which affect a game other than those by a player. (Note that nature is sometimes described as a player in the game, but we are making a distinction for simplicity.) For the purposes of analysis, one could consider the less important players to be part of nature.

States in the Cybersecurity Game

The state of the cybersecurity game contains all information relevant to the current situation in the game, including the past history of the game. As the game progresses, it moves from one state to another. It is not possible to describe the state of the cybersecurity game fully due to the large amount of relevant information. Instead, we will give examples of different types of information contained in the game's state. That information includes the following:

- The resources available to each player

- The current state of all cyber assets

- The knowledge and beliefs of each player

- Current laws related to cybersecurity

- The history of actions by attackers, defenders, and law enforcement

From those examples alone, it is clear that the cybersecurity game's state contains an unwieldly amount of information. For the purposes of practical analysis, only the most important information is considered. The examples in the next chapter illustrate how to reduce the game's state to a reasonable amount of information.

Actions in the Cybersecurity Game

The cybersecurity game is a simultaneous game. Actions occur in real time, and players are unaware of the actions of most other players. The actions available depend on the state of the game. Examples of actions are the following:

- A player accruing resources such as personnel

- An attacker selecting a target

- A defender securing cyber assets

- Conducting or responding to a cyberattack

- Developing cybersecurity products

- Passing and enforcing cybersecurity laws

Note that some of the preceding actions are long-term, and some are short-term. Recruiting personnel, setting up defenses of cyber assets, and passing laws are long-term actions with long-term consequences. Selecting targets, conducting a cyberattack, and responding to an immediate cyberattack are short-term actions with immediate consequences.

Payoffs in the Cybersecurity Game

A payoff is a gain or loss for a player in a game. In the cybersecurity game, we will consider payoffs to be equivalent to an amount of currency. It may not be obvious how to convert different types of gains or losses into currency. The following examples illustrate how that could be done. We referenced before an attacker who engages in cyberattacks for fun. There is probably an amount of currency, either a positive gain or a negative loss, that would convince the attacker to cease. That amount of currency would be the equivalent of fun for that attacker. Nation-states typically pursue strategic objectives. There is a maximum amount of currency a nation-state would be willing or able to invest in order to ensure attaining an objective. That amount of currency is the financial equivalent of the objective.

Every expenditure of money, time, or resources is a negative payoff. Attackers only realize positive payoffs after a successful attack. Rational attackers attempt to maximize net payoff. Investing in cybersecurity is a negative payoff for defenders, but the intention is to eliminate or reduce losses from successful cyberattacks. Rational defenders attempt to minimize losses.

Payoffs for other players are more difficult to model. One could consider earnings to be the payoff for cybersecurity providers, but that is blending the cybersecurity game with an economic game. One possibility for determining government payoffs is to consider long-term tax revenue. In that model, a rational government would address cybersecurity in the way that would maximize corporate and individual tax revenue over time.

The preceding discussion referenced how rational players would act. Not every player in the cybersecurity game is rational. Players may not understand which actions are in their best interest, or players may disregard payoffs altogether. Any analysis must account for the possibility of irrational players.

Knowledge and Beliefs in the Cybersecurity Game

The cybersecurity game is a game of incomplete and imperfect information. Essentially, players in the cybersecurity game are ignorant of much information: the number and identity of other players, the state of the game, the strategies of other players, the payoffs of other players, etc. Certain types of information can be especially valuable. For example, if an attacker has inside knowledge about a defender, a successful attack is more likely. If a defender has knowledge about the number and types of attackers who will target that defender, then the defender can more optimally allocate resources.

Since knowledge is limited in the cybersecurity game, we will introduce the notion of belief. For our purposes, a player's beliefs contain all of the player's knowledge together with all of the player's assumptions. To be mathematically precise, assumptions would be modeled with a probability distribution. For example, suppose an attacker estimates a payoff of $10,000 from a successful attack against a defender. That could be modeled using a normal distribution with mean $10,000 and some specified variance. In practice, the attacker may express the assumption more simply. A payoff within the range of $7,500–$12,500 could be within the attacker's expectation, but the attacker would be surprised to receive a payoff of only $1,000.

Generally, a player's beliefs contain some level of inaccuracy. Also, note that beliefs can change frequently. As a player gains more information, that player will also update related assumptions. Finally, beliefs can be either explicit or implicit. If we assume that a player is rational, we can infer a range of underlying beliefs from the player's strategy.

We will now give some examples of common beliefs. When an attacker assesses a defender, the attacker makes several assumptions: the probability of success of an attack, the time and resources required to execute an attack, and the likely payoff if the attack is successful. Defenders make similar assumptions: the types of likely attackers, the probability of a successful attack, and the damages from a successful attack. The cost-benefit analysis discussed in Chapter 3 depends on the beliefs of the player. Inaccurate beliefs lead to faulty analysis, which can lead to a significant reduction in payoff.

Now, we will clarify why this concept is essential. The strategy of the players in the cybersecurity game depends on the beliefs of the players. If it is possible to influence a player's beliefs, then it is also possible to influence that player's strategy. If an attacker believes that it is unprofitable to attack a defender (or that it is more profitable to attack another defender), then a rational attacker will not even make an attempt against that defender.

That introduces the concept of reputation. We will define reputation as the set of beliefs other players have about a specified player. That includes information about the player's resources, payoffs, and strategy. A player can attempt to create a specific reputation by taking calculated actions. For example, law enforcement can strongly pursue every attacker who targets critical infrastructure. That increases the possibility of criminal or civil penalties for an attacker, thus making it less profitable to attack those targets.

Modeling the Cybersecurity Game

Constructing a realistic model of the entire cybersecurity game would require collecting a large amount of data. It would also require many assumptions to fill in missing information. First, the players would need to be identified. Some players could be identified using public information: governments, cybersecurity providers, and high-profile defenders (such as corporations). Low-profile defenders, such as individuals with personal computers, would be harder to identify, but the number could be estimated.

Attackers are much harder to identify. The number and types of attackers could be estimated by using information from known cyberattacks. Multiple attackers with similar strategies could be treated as a single player for the purposes of the game theory model. Since this approach does not consider unknown attacks, the estimate based on known attacks could be highly inaccurate.

Collecting information about resources, payoffs, beliefs, and strategies of players would be even more difficult. Constructing a full, realistic model is impractical for most applications. For the purposes of analysis, models are constructed using many simplifying assumptions. Examples are given in the next sections and the next chapter.

Analysis of the Cybersecurity Game

We will use the following problem to illustrate analysis of cybersecurity using game theory. Suppose there is a group of similar corporations who all meet the same cybersecurity standard. In game theory terms, an attacker would expect similar costs to attack each corporation and similar gains upon success. We will analyze the effects of corporations upgrading their cybersecurity above the standard or downgrading it below the standard.

Our example game contains one attacker and six defenders. Each defender will choose whether to maintain the standard level of cybersecurity, upgrade, or downgrade. Then, the attacker will launch attacks against three of the defenders. We will assume that four of the defenders maintain the same level of security, one upgrades, and one downgrades. Now, we will define the game state from the attacker's perspective.

The attacker must pay a fixed cost to complete an attack against each defender. The cost is −5 for the defenders who maintained the standard level of security, −10 for the defender who upgraded, and −1 for the defender who downgraded. From the attacker's perspective, the gain is approximately 100 for each defender. The information is summarized in Figure 9-4.

Defender	Cost	Gain	Net Payoff
A	-10	100	90
B	-5	100	95
C	-5	100	95
D	-5	100	95
E	-5	100	95
F	-1	100	99

Figure 9-4. *Attacker's Net Payoff from Attacking Each Defender*

A rational attacker would attack defender F and choose two targets randomly from defenders B, C, D, and E. Even though it is profitable to attack defender A, it is more profitable to attack the other defenders. Therefore, upgrading cybersecurity discouraged the attack from occurring, and down-grading made the attack a certainty. Now, we must translate our analysis into a hypothesis about cybersecurity. We will illustrate how not to do this first in order to make an important point.

Absurd Hypothesis: Corporations who exceed the standard for cybersecurity will never be attacked, and corporations who have substandard cybersecurity will always be attacked first.

The problem with this hypothesis is that it does not incorporate the assumptions of the model. Because the model is greatly simplified, there are many assumptions. Some of the relevant assumptions are the following:

- The attacker cannot complete attacks against every defender.

- The attacker is aware of the level of cybersecurity for each defender.

- The attacker is rational.

- The attacker considers net gain when discriminating among targets.

The first assumption is plausible. Assuming each attack requires a considerable amount of time, an attacker must choose which defenders to target and which to ignore. The second assumption is an important addition to the hypothesis. The upgrades and downgrades to cybersecurity must be apparent to an attacker in order to influence the attacker's behavior. The third and fourth assumptions are true in some cases, but not in others. If we assume that a significant percentage of attackers are rational and consider net gain, then the game still implies a change in attacker behavior overall. Therefore, we can formulate the following hypothesis.

Hypothesis: If upgrades or downgrades are apparent to an attacker, corporations who exceed the standard for cybersecurity are less likely to be attacked, and corporations who have substandard cybersecurity are more likely to be attacked.

This hypothesis is important because it suggests a dual benefit from investing in cybersecurity. Not only does improving cybersecurity make attacks less likely to succeed but it also makes them less likely to occur. Thus, improved cybersecurity will have a greater benefit than expected.

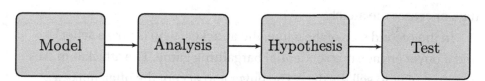

Figure 9-5. *Steps to Apply Game Theory to Cybersecurity*

We still cannot assert that the hypothesis is correct. Any conclusion is only as valid as the underlying assumptions. In a game as complicated as the cybersecurity game, it is not possible to identify and evaluate every assumption. Therefore, the hypothesis must be tested in practice. By collecting data about attacks against similar corporations with different levels of cybersecurity, statistics would either support or contradict the hypothesis.

This example showed how to apply game theory to cybersecurity practically. Construct a simplified model to study the topic of interest, and analyze that model. Make a hypothesis based on that analysis which incorporates the relevant assumptions. Finally, test the hypothesis to determine whether it is valid in practice. The process is summarized in Figure 9-5.

Subgame Analysis

The next chapter outlines a game which can be separated into multiple discrete steps. Analysis of the entire game can be simplified by analyzing each subgame, starting at the end of the game. We will illustrate this with a simple example.

The first step of our example game involves two players, an attacker and a defender. The attacker launches a cyberattack against the defender in order to gain access to valuable data. The attacker utilizes a series of actions in order to attain the goal. The defender may or may not respond to the cyberattack in progress. Ultimately, the attacker either acquires the data or ceases the attack.

In the second step of the game, the attacker (who is now a seller) and a buyer engage in a sequential bargaining game. The attacker makes an initial offer to sell the data. The buyer can accept the offer, make a counteroffer, or cease negotiations. Alternating counteroffers continue until one player either accepts the offer or stops bargaining. The attacker's net payoff from the entire game is the revenue from the data minus the cost of the cyberattack and the cost of bargaining. The game from the attacker's point of view is summarized in Figure 9-6.

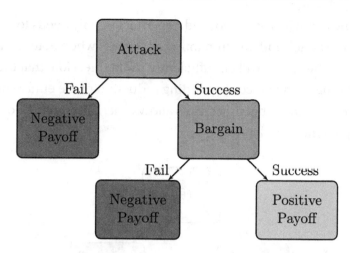

Figure 9-6. *Game from the Attacker's Point of View*

The bargaining step is an example of a subgame. Once the attacker has acquired the data, the sequential bargaining game can be analyzed independently without considering the step that preceded it. Now, we will clarify why this concept is useful. When determining whether or not to initiate or continue the cyberattack, the attacker must consider both the attack step and the bargaining step of the game. This analysis can be simplified by reducing the bargaining subgame to its expected payoff.

Based on the attacker's beliefs, the attacker can estimate the likely outcomes of the bargaining subgame. To be precise, this estimate would be represented with a probability distribution. Instead, we will assume that the attacker is only concerned about the expected value. Regardless of how the attacker performs the analysis, the bargaining subgame can be reduced to a single expected payoff. The reduced game is represented in Figure 9-7.

Once the game has been reduced, the attacker only needs to consider the cost of the attack and the probability of success when determining whether the cyberattack will be sufficiently profitable. Note that the analysis of subgames and corresponding reduction of the entire game can be repeated any number of times. This allows each discrete step of a game to be analyzed independently.

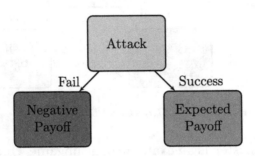

Figure 9-7. *Reduced Game from the Attacker's Point of View*

CHAPTER 10

Game Theory Case Study: Ransomware

Introduction

Game theory is an excellent tool for analyzing complex, competitive situations. Cybersecurity is concerned with just such situations involving attackers, defenders, and others like regulating entities. Within game theory, "a particular game is defined when the choices open to the players in each situation, the situations defining the end of play, and the payoffs associated with each play-terminating situation have been specified."[1] This does not apply to a general cybersecurity situation. We use the term "infinite game" to describe something like a game such that: players may start or stop playing the game at any time; the end of play may never be defined; and the rules governing play may change at any time without all (or any) players knowing about the changes. While infinite games do not meet the strict definition of a game, both games and infinite games can be analyzed with the rigor and tools of game theory.

To analyze ransomware attacks as part of the infinite cybersecurity game, we describe and analyze several games (in the strict game theory sense) and discuss how these games relate to the infinite game.

---

[1] Rapoport, Anatol. Two-person Game Theory. Courier Corporation, 1999.

© Dr. Jacob G. Oakley, Michael Butler, Wayne York, Dr. Matthew Puckett, Dr. J. Louis Sewell 2022
J. G. Oakley et al., *Theoretical Cybersecurity*, https://doi.org/10.1007/978-1-4842-8300-4_10

Our focus is on enabling the reader to understand the value of applying game theory techniques to real cybersecurity problems. Some of the techniques discussed in the previous chapter are applied here to situations from a defender's perspective, and some from an attacker's perspective.

In all cases, the applications are intended to help the reader make better security-focused decisions. This does not mean the applications will all be in the cybersecurity domain. For example, understanding applications of game theory to negotiations is an important tool for minimizing the payment a defender will be required to give an attacker. The expected value of such payments, together with the likelihood of ending up in such a negotiation and many other considerations, can be used to accurately reason over potential ransomware attack outcomes. Of course, the level of accuracy depends on the data available to estimate certain unknown quantities. Here, a government agency, such as the FBI, can be instrumental in helping estimate these quantities in order to perform a proper analysis.

A simplified version of the global problem of ransomware is modeled as involving the steps outlined as follows. While no single ransomware attack will involve all the steps that follow, each step is relevant to a possible ransomware attack. Also, some of these steps may occur simultaneously or in very quick succession. For example, payload activation and making a ransom demand may happen together. Note that while there are many effects that could be considered during the payload activation step, we narrow our attention to data encryption only.

- **Attack capability development.** The attacker develops, purchases, or otherwise obtains the ability to implement some attacker steps of a ransomware attack. For example, this may include the ability to detect whether a defender has initiated a cybersecurity mitigation measure after the payload has been activated.

- **Defense capability development.** The defender implements security measures to mitigate the threat of a ransomware attack and enables some defender steps of a ransomware attack. For example, this may include the ability to recover data from a backup.

- **Target selection.** The attacker determines whether to attack the defender and, if so, which defender information systems to target.

- **Payload deployment.** This involves initial access to an information system, network discovery, vulnerability exploitation, and many other activities normally associated with a cybersecurity attack of an information system. The end result of this is a deployed payload and the ability to activate the payload.

- **Payload activation.** A portion of the information is disabled via data encryption.

- **Ransom demand.** The ransom demand is presented to the target.

- **Cybersecurity mitigation.** The defender recovers or replaces the data without receiving the encryption key from the attacker.

- **Retaliation.** If a mitigation attempt is detected, the attacker renders further damage and permanently withholds the key.

- **Ransom response.** The defender decides whether to pay the ransom demand, enter into negotiations with the attacker, or neither.

- **Payoff negotiation.** The defender and attacker negotiate terms of a ransom payoff.

- **Payoff.** The terms of the ransom payoff are enacted or
  bluffed. This may include providing the encryption key,
  paying the negotiated payoff amount, or both.

- **Recovery.** The defender takes measures to ensure
  the payoff deactivation is complete, the data is usable
  and uncorrupted, the payload itself is wiped from
  the information system, and the information system
  vulnerabilities that allowed payload deployment are
  patched or otherwise mitigated.

It is beyond the current scope to give a complete analysis that
thoroughly considers each step. Instead, we examine only certain steps in
isolation or in combination with each other. Our aim is to help the reader
gain an intuition for the kind of considerations involved in a game theory
analysis and to enable the reader to understand the value of applying game
theory techniques to real cybersecurity problems.

In addition to considering steps in combination, it is valuable to
consider attacks in combination. One ransomware attack involves one
attacker entity (person, state, group, etc.) and one defender entity. Many
ransomware attacks involving the same attacker may take place in concert
with each other. For a complete analysis, it is important to consider many
potential attacker and defender types. Likewise, it is important to consider
many attacks that may occur simultaneously or in sequence rather than
just a single attack in isolation.

Our exploration starts with the final step involving a simple
attacker versus defender game arrived at via a number of simplifying
assumptions. This approach provides the analyst with results that assist
with understanding more realistic behaviors in a more complex scenario.
Throughout the chapter, we introduce additional complexity as we include
additional steps in reverse order. When analyzing earlier steps, this
approach allows us to treat later steps as a subgame that can be summarized
with expected values of outcomes, as presented in the previous chapter.

Payoff and Recovery

The first step we consider is the payoff. In this step, the attacker and defender both take actions. The payoff negotiation could include any variety of potential actions for either side. For now, we assume the agreement is two-fold. First, if the defender provides a payment of the agreed amount, then the attacker will provide an encryption key that will allow the defender to recover their data. Second, if the defender does not provide the payment of the agreed amount by the agreed time, the attacker – as punishment for not upholding the agreement – will permanently withhold the encryption key. The potential actions and outcomes for this game are shown in Figure 10-1. The outcomes are described in terms of attacker and defender payoffs.

Looking at this game in isolation, there is no incentive for the attacker to give the key after the defender provides the payment. That is, the payment to the attacker is the same whether the key is provided or not.

However, if the key is not provided, then the attacker can immediately return to the ransom demand step to try to get an additional payment. For the attacker who is not concerned about reputation, there is no downside to this.

Regardless of whether the key is provided, the recovery step is critical to preventing the attacker from reactivating the payload – which may survive a data wipe – at a later time.

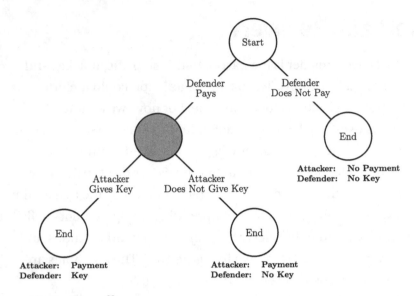

Figure 10-1. *Payoff game*

Reputation

Let's take a closer look at the role of reputation, beginning with the game presented in Section Payoff and Recovery. Before deciding whether to pay, the defender has some belief about how the attacker would respond were a payment provided. (Even if the defender does not actually have a belief about this, this can be modelled mathematically as having an equal belief in each possible outcome.) If the belief that the attacker will not provide the key is strong enough, then this belief justifies the defender withholding payment. In this case, justification for the belief itself ultimately determines how justified the defender is in withholding payment.

For this reason, the attacker may choose to care about reputation. For reputation to matter to the attacker, there must be a way for subsequent defenders targeted by the attacker to know or at least form beliefs about the outcome of the current payoff. This may happen via government-provided statistics on ransomware payoffs in general. It may happen via statistics associated with this specific attacker. In this latter case, the attacker would have to establish an identity and make that identity known at some step prior to the payoff step.

This identity, or rather the marker of the identity, now presents an opportunity to other attackers. Let's say the attacker so far is attacker A, who wants to have a reputation of honoring the terms of the payoff negotiation. Suppose there is an attacker who is motivated to withhold the key. For example, consider attacker B, who wants to take advantage of A's reputation. If B can use the same marker of identity used by A, then B can masquerade as A. Then, when it comes to a payoff structure like Figure 10-1, B can reap the benefits of A's reputation. That is, despite B having no intention of providing the key, the defender may still pay because A has a strong reputation of honoring the terms agreed to in the previous step.

Is it in B's interest to withhold the key in this case? That depends on B's goals, which may be incompatible with A's goals. If B wants to cause chaos or has a grudge against the defender, then it may be worth it to B to withhold the key and allow A's reputation to change because of it. If B wants to make as much money as possible over the course of many attacks, it may be worth it to B to provide the key in such situations to keep A's reputation strong. There very well could be situations in which there is a high cost of building a reputation, but maintaining one carries no cost and has other benefits. This would explain why B would masquerade as A rather than just build a reputation independently.

Now suppose B is a nation state and wants to inflict as much damage on another nation as possible. Here, B's strategy is to target defenders in the opposing nation and masquerade as A to take payments without providing keys to defenders. Masquerading allows for a high chance of receiving payments without incurring the cost of building a reputation. Receiving payments and withholding keys damages the opposing nation.

For this analysis, we simplify by holding fixed the cost of getting to the payoff step while masquerading as attacker A and the structure of the payoff game (fixed to that of Figure 10-1). To make calculations quite easy, we also simplify our model of A's reputation and our model of the defender. A's reputation is a number between zero and one calculated as a ratio. The top of the ratio is the total number of times A or B has provided the key to a defender. The bottom of the ratio is the total number of times A or B has been paid by a defender. The defender will pay if the reputation of A is above a threshold and will not pay otherwise. The primary variable is whether B will provide a key after the defender has provided payment.

Suppose A has been paid by a large number of defenders and has stopped attacking altogether. Before B's first attack, A's reputation is one. Once B starts attacking, A's reputation drops more or less quickly depending on how often B withholds the key from a defender. Figure 10-2 shows three possibilities. The solid line shows the reputation decay if B withholds the key for every defender. This quickly drops below the threshold for the defender providing a payment. The dotted line shows the decay if B withholds the key for every other defender. This drops below the threshold more slowly. If B provides the key for a percentage of defenders that matches the threshold, A's reputation never drops below the threshold. This represents nearly the greatest damage B can do to the opposing nation in this simplified scenario.

There is a much richer depth of reputation analysis possible even for this question of how often to provide or withhold the key from a defender; more so when including all the steps of a ransomware attack. Indeed, the analysis presented is embarrassingly oversimplified. Proper analysis requires more advanced techniques and the relaxation of simplifying assumptions. While this deeper analysis is beyond the scope of this work, the fact that this analysis could be done is immanently relevant. Considering reputation over sequences of attacks is more realistic and more complex. The results of a proper analysis offer a great advantage to whichever players (attacker, defender, or regulator) obtain them. Given the expertise (i.e., expense) required to do this, it is likely only justifiable for very large corporations, very large criminal organizations, or nation-states (which includes attackers, defenders, and regulators) to conduct.

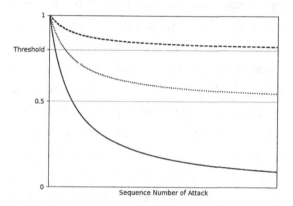

Figure 10-2. *Reputation Decay*

Payoff Negotiation

A proper treatment of game theory concepts for negotiation is well beyond the scope of this work. Whole textbooks have been written on just this topic. Instead, we consider how to incorporate an important finding of the payoff step analysis into the strategy for payoff negotiation. Here, the players' strategies consist of three elements: the structure of the payoff step, the terms the attacker agrees to enact, and the terms the defender agrees to enact.

The structure of the game of Figure 10-1 that puts the defender at a particular disadvantage is the sequential nature of the payoffs. The defender makes a payment or not. Even after a payment is made, the attacker is free to choose to provide the key or change a prior decision about providing the key.

Taking this into account, the payoff negotiation should have a different expected outcome for payoff structures that permit payoff terms to be fulfilled sequentially versus structures that employ one of the many protocols for simultaneous implementation of terms.

In considering ransomware steps that occur before negotiation, we can treat negotiation and payoff as a subgame that can be reduced to expected values over possible outcomes. The significant outcome variations to consider will include the attacker providing the encryption key and the attacker not providing the key. For example, in the response game of Figure 10-3, the left, gray node is the beginning of this subgame. The child nodes of this are the two significant outcome variations just described. One represents the average overall negotiations and payoffs that include the attacker providing the encryption key, the other that do not include providing the key. The payments associated with these child nodes are expected values based on a full analysis of the subgame.

Note well that to calculate the expected values for a summarized game, the likelihood of each outcome must be calculated (or at least estimated). This is best done by considering reputation and beliefs of the players.

Ransom Response, Mitigation, and Retaliation

Once the ransom demand has been made, it is up to the defender to decide whether to engage the demand, try to mitigate the damage, or just to accept the loss of data. As mentioned before, we simplify the sub-games by representing only the expected value of outcomes. Here, the important outcomes cover cases in which the key is provided or not, different payment amounts are provided, different amounts of effort are spent, and whether the attacker successfully inflicts additional damage.

The effort required by a player refers to the effort required to negotiate or mitigate. To make the example manageable, we assume the effort required is similar for all negotiations, is similar but different for all mitigation outcomes, and is zero when not negotiating or mitigating. In the language of the previous chapter, effort is a kind of cost. There may be other kinds of cost to consider, too.

The additional damage an attacker may inflict is relevant only when the defender attempts to mitigate the attack instead of negotiate. This damage may be as simple as corrupting or deleting the encrypted data. This is relevant if the defender does not pair the mitigation attempt with a successful recovery step or if the defender tries to recoup value from the encrypted data (like waiting until quantum computers can crack the encryption). It is not relevant if the defender recovers the data via another means (like a backup) and successfully implements a recovery step.

The salient outcome possibilities are shown in Figure 10-3.

To reason over these outcomes, the players must have a way to rank the outcomes. One way is to convert the outcome types into common units of payoff for each player. However, it is not necessary to have a formula that produces a single number to be used for the ranking. Such a formula that has certain properties is called a von Neumann-Morgenstern utility function and is useful for a great many game-theoretic techniques involving rationality, risk aversion, expected utility, and more. In the language of the previous chapter, utility is equivalent to payoff.

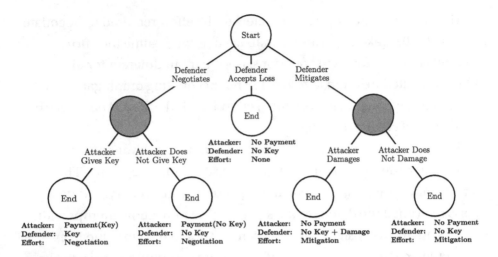

Figure 10-3. *Response game*

Having such a function available is common in this situation. This is because cybersecurity decisions relevant to ransomware attacks are often phrased in terms of monetary cost. This means the cost of having or not having the encryption key and of expending a negotiation- or mitigation-level of effort are explicitly converted into expected dollar amounts. Even when schedule is an important cost to consider, the impact of schedule can often be converted into an equivalent monetary cost. A formula that produces a monetary cost for each outcome can be treated as a von Neumann-Morgenstern utility function.

In the absence of a von Neumann-Morgenstern utility function, simply having a ranking of the outcomes provides the foundation to apply quite powerful game theory tools that enable excellent insights into optimal choices and expected behavior. For a complete analysis based on rankings alone, each player must know or estimate the outcome rankings of all players. There is an important variation on this in which explicit rankings are not known or estimated, but the belief about different rankings is known. This also provides the necessary foundation for a robust game-theoretic analysis.

One insight from this outcome-ranking consideration is that the defender can only be expected to negotiate if the effort required to negotiate is not too high and the chance of a mitigation attempt being successful is not too high. To be more precise, it is the defender's belief about this effort and chance that matter most. Carefully considering beliefs and reputation come into play in calculating or estimating these.

As the subgames of the response game were summarized using expected values, the response game itself is a subgame of a larger game. Based on the goal of a larger analysis, this can be summarized a number of ways. In one sense, the game cannot be simplified as the outcomes each have a unique combination of key/no key/damage and level of effort. However, if the focus of analysis is on the value of mitigation, it would be useful to summarize the game into two outcomes given as expected cost when the defender mitigates or does not mitigate. This kind of analysis would help justify a potential defender spending money on cybersecurity mitigation equipment, software, and personnel prior to a ransomware attack.

Activation and Demand

We assume activation and demand steps occur near-simultaneously, so they can be considered together as one step. To simplify further, consider a situation in which the presentation of a demand to even one defender leads to a widespread update to antivirus signatures that would render further attempts to deploy payloads unlikely to succeed.

In this idealized (and admittedly unrealistic) case, an attacker can choose to activate payloads at different times. This may help space out the load on resources required for negotiation and payoff steps. However, the more time passes between deployment and activation for a given defender, the more likely that defender will discover and remove the payload prior to activation. As the number of deployed payloads increases, the elapsed time between the first and last activated payload increases, resulting in an increase in the chance of a defender discovering and removing the last payload to be activated. This diminishing return limits the maximum expected value of the number of payments an attacker will receive.

In a more realistic case, an attacker is not limited to a single or even a fixed number of deployment techniques. There are also techniques that are not thwarted by software of any kind – for example, exploiting humans to compromise the network. Still, the lesson of the idealized case applies. Once a payload is deployed, it is in the attacker's interest to activate it before too much time passes.

Notice the analysis of this step is about optimizing expected payment for the attacker. In this sense, it is an optimization analysis, not a game-theoretic analysis. It does depend on game theory analysis, though. This is because the determination of expected value of payment relies on the game theory analysis of steps that come after deployment and activation and demand steps. This mix of analysis types is common in evaluating complex games.

Deployment

Deployment involves initial access to an information system, network discovery, vulnerability exploitation, and many other activities normally associated with a cybersecurity attack of an information system. As with negotiation, a proper treatment of game theory concepts for Deployment is beyond the scope of this work, as the research in this area goes back decades.

Of particular interest and usefulness are the graph-based methods. A graph is a collection of nodes with edges between the nodes. A protected network can be modelled as a graph with each asset (router, domain controller, host, etc.) represented as a node and steps in an attack path from one node to another represented as directed edges. These nodes and edges can be imbued with amplifying information, such as installed software, known exploits, firewall rules, etc.. Such a graph can be used to perform a static analysis of the overall level of security of a network, perform a dynamic assessment of the risk of a specific set of assets being compromised given real-time alerts, and provide a great deal of insight of many other kinds.

For the current work, the details of such analyses are less important than knowing they can be carried out in a structured, meaningful manner. We can model this step as having two outcomes, the attacker is successful or not successful in deploying the payload. Both of these outcomes can be associated with a probability, defender cost, and attacker cost.

On the defender side, these probabilities are primarily based on the specific network being compromised (it's topology, controls, policies, vulnerabilities, etc.), the manner in which the network is protected (as determined by the defender's capability development step), and the skill of the people monitoring and protecting the network. On the attacker side, these probabilities are primarily based on the specific network being compromised, the manner in which the network is attacked (as determined by the attacker's capability development step), and the skill of the people monitoring and attacking the network.

Selection

At this step, there are no defenders, only potential defenders. In this sense, while the ransomware attack has begun, the ransomware game (in the game theory sense) has not begun. That is, the infinite ransomware game (itself a sub-infinite-game of the infinite cybersecurity game) has begun, but the strict conditions for a game have not yet been met.

A number of factors could be considered here. How much financial liquidity does a potential defender have? How good is their network security? How well-trained are the people using or protecting the network?

Which software or configuration vulnerabilities are unmitigated? How likely are they to hire a professional negotiator or turn to the FBI for help? While all of these considerations, and many more, are relevant, they can be difficult or impossible to assess prior to the deployment step.

The attacker's capabilities may dictate the deployment method. In turn, this may dictate or restrict the selection criteria. For example, an attacker may choose to compromise a security information and event management (SIEM) product. In this case, the potential defenders available to be attacked are limited to those who utilize the compromised SIEM.

To conduct a high-quality analysis of the ransomware game as a whole, it is necessary to collect and incorporate statistics on the methods used to deploy payloads. This can help the analyst better understand the selection step. The goal of analysis here is to understand the conditions that make it more or less likely to be selected for an attack.

Capability Development

Attacker capability development involves developing, buying, training, or otherwise obtaining the skills and tools necessary to perform each of the steps of a ransomware attack. Defender capability development involves obtaining the skills and tools necessary to defend against a ransomware attack. We examine how the different steps of a ransomware attack inform the decisions made during capability development. While we focus on the defender's decisions, we will consider some attacker decisions along the way.

Deployment

This is where the bulk of the budget is spent for a cybersecurity operations center. Selecting a SIEM, an antivirus solution, personnel, training, policies, security controls, and much more comes into play. Even scratching the surface of the mass of considerations for this is beyond the scope of this work. In aggregate, these decisions impact the likelihood that a randomly selected defender will succumb to the exploits of the attacker during payload deployment.

Activation, Demand, Mitigation, Retaliation, Recovery

At this point in the attack, the network is compromised. The defender has failed to prevent the data from being encrypted against the defender's will. Whether or not the demand has been made, the defender can cut the overall attack short and minimize the impact of the attack by detecting and mitigating the encryption.

The mitigation may involve restoring data from a backup, using a separate fail-over network with duplicate data, or a variety of other solutions – all of which can be cost-justified if the threat of ransomware attacks becomes too great. Regardless of the mitigation, there is the threat of retaliation. We assume the attacker can at least delete the data that is encrypted. Undoubtedly, there is more the attacker can delete and corrupt. If all that can be affected by the attacker is covered by the mitigation plan, then retaliation is an empty threat. Implicit in this condition is that the mitigation plan includes a full recovery plan. Otherwise, the attacker may be able to reactivate or redeploy with minimal effort and a higher demanded payment.

Response, Negotiation, Payoff

If mitigation is not an option, the response options are to accept the loss or negotiate. At this point, the most notable aspect of capability development that may help is training in negotiation tactics, not a cybersecurity discipline.

Attacker Types

Before getting to the target selection step, we consider four types of attackers. First, there is the low-capability attacker. They can only take advantage of defenders who have not provided a minimum foundation of protection.

Next, there is the high-capability attacker. This could range from the cyber arm of an organized crime operation to a very capable individual. This type of attacker can develop robust capabilities and use them to compromise a target network. These attackers are a real threat to any organization.

The third type is the optimized attacker. This is a high-capability attacker who designs campaigns to optimize the use of resources. This is distinct from the high-capability capability attacker who may attack opportunistically without regard for the efficient use of resources. In game theory terms, the optimized attacker is a rational player – this is a technical term defined mathematically. Contrasting this, the (non-optimized) high-capability attacker is either non-rational or has bounded rationality.

Finally, we have the APT attacker. This can be a high-capability attacker or an optimized attacker. The distinguishing feature is the APT attacker has a very high budget of time and money, whereas the other attacker types are comparatively quite limited.

In terms of the 1-9-90 principle in Chapter 3, the APT attacker is the 1, the high-capability and optimized attackers are the 9, and the low-capability attacker is the 90.

Target Selection

Here, we ask the question, "how can the likelihood of attack be minimized?" We consider one aspect of this with a simplified game. The purpose of this game is to demonstrate the weakness of only considering aggregate probabilities in analyzing potential cybersecurity outcomes.

To narrow our focus, we look at options for selecting software to protect a network. Intentionally leaving the type of software vague, suppose there are three options. Each option has different levels of cost, popularity, and provided security, as shown in Table 10-1.

Suppose a new defender is making a cybersecurity plan and needs to select one of these options. We assume the popularity of each option is sufficiently high that the defender's choice will have a negligible effect on popularity. We also assume the cost of each option is within the budget of the defender. Next, we consider the security of each option.

Here, it is useful to recall the chapter on Infinite Cybersecurity (Chapter 8). The key lesson to apply here is that the defender should not try to "win" the cybersecurity game. This applies equally to ransomware attacks and other types of attacks. Rather, the defender should try to keep playing as long as possible. To this end, the software options can help the defender capitalize on the access to and information of their own attack surface, systems, and organization.

Table 10-1. *Attributes of software options for network protection*

Option	Cost	Popularity	Security
A	High	Medium	High
B	Medium	High	Highest
C	Low	Low	Medium

We assume that no software choice will make a defender protected against APT threats. This is a cost of playing the infinite game that must be accepted. Software option C provides for the minimum foundation needed to protect against low-capability attackers – when coupled with capable and well-trained professionals (a must that is often overlooked even for the highest-budget operations centers). Software options A and B provide good protection against low- and high-capability attacker types when coupled with capable and well-trained professionals. The difference is that option B has a greater record of success. Keep in mind that this record is in an aggregate measure that does not take into account the frequency of each attacker type. When thinking only about this record of success versus cost, the defender has a clear reason to select option B, as it dominates option A in cost and security.

The most interesting case to consider is the optimized attacker. This attacker wants to optimize their gain per unit of effort. How popularity and security compare with each other numerically determines the optimal choice for the optimized attacker. In this sense, the security value for the software options can be thought of as the level of effort required by the attacker to circumvent or otherwise thwart the software. If the attacker can find or develop an exploit for either option A or option B, then they can pursue attacks against a large part of the population of users for the affected software.

Suppose the effort required to compromise option B is twice that to compromise option A and the number of users of option B is ten-fold greater than the number of users of option A. In this case, the optimized attacker is justified in targeting users of option B if the expected value of payoff is the same for targeting a user of option A and targeting a user of option B. Assuming these expected values are the same, compromising option B gives a 5-fold yield vs. compromising option A (twice the effort for ten times the payoff). Strictly speaking, the attacker's beliefs about popularity, level of effort, and expected payoffs are more important than the actual values.

From the defender's perspective, this insight about the optimized attacker may change the risk assessment for each option. As we have already pointed out, the defender can calculate or estimate the equivalent cost of compromise weighted by the likelihood of being targeted. Now, the defender has to reason over the chance that selecting a more popular software option increases the likelihood of being targeted. This may well outweigh the cost savings for selecting option B over option A.

It is critical in these situations to ensure the basic foundation of security is not compromised on the basis of a popularity argument. That is, if option A's high level of security is just not high enough, then the defender is justified in selecting option B even if this comes with an increased likelihood of being targeted by optimized attackers.

Before leaving this example, we draw a comparison to another decision about how a cybersecurity budget could be spent. In this example, the main decision was about a trade-off between cost, security, and likelihood of being targeted. This same kind of analysis can be used to decide between using high-cost software (like a SIEM) with median-capability staff versus using the same software with high-capability staff. The increased cost in training or salaries can be offset by a lower expected value of the cost of compromise. This lower compromise cost comes from lowering the probability of being compromised.

Summary

We introduced one variation of a ransomware attack and analyzed it using game-theoretic and optimization methods. The presented techniques include a small sample of game theory tools for a skilled analyst to apply. The overall analysis was broken down into smaller analysis steps that were combined together into higher-level analyses incrementally. This required us to consider steps of a ransomware attack in reverse order, where the smallest games to analyze involve the final steps of an attack.

To get the best results, a multitude of aspects must be properly considered. One of the most subtle and difficult aspects to handle rightly is reputation. However, this is especially important for regulators to consider so that the regulations they impose will have a chance of yielding the effects intended.

Another subtle and difficult aspect to consider is the type of attackers. The proper incorporation of this concept requires understanding the methods, reasons, beliefs, and rationality of the attacker types. In addition, the number of each type is important to take into account. However, the number of each type may be difficult to determine. Thus, this kind of information may only be available via nation-state-level entities.

Two areas of research that we were not able to present in depth are the game theory of negotiation and attack graphs. These require great knowledge and skill to apply correctly. However, they offer excellent value when properly applied to the analysis of ransomware attacks or of cybersecurity in general.

A major goal of this work is to enable readers to make disciplined choices about how to use available resources. For the cybersecurity professional, this includes the time and budget within the given scope. For the executive, this includes taking into account the likelihood and severity of outcomes as a function of how much the cybersecurity budget is increased or how restrictions are put on the use of this budget. In either case, reasoning over costs, outcomes, and risk can be significantly aided using the robust tools of game theory.

Index

A

Addressing defensible security assessments, 98

Addressing defensible systems administration, 99

Advanced persistent threat (APT), 13

Adversary as a Service (AaaS), 156, 157

Antagonist functions, 31

APT attacker, 200

APT emulation, 99

Assessor recommendations, 82

Attacker capability development
attacker types, 200
demand, 199
mitigation, 199
payload deployment, 199
response options, 199
retaliation and recovery, 199
target selection, 201–204

Auditing, 144, 145

Automated communication with TCP port randomization prevention, 11

Automated worm with bad automation logic, 14

B

Bad cost benefit, 39

Box thinking, 68

Business intelligence professional, 35

Business strategy, 66

By-mail scams, 56

C

CAPTR Reporting
cost benefit, 118–124
mathematical analysis, 117
safety, 116
web/reverse risk relationships, 117, 118

CAPTR team engagement, 105, 110, 119

CAPTR teamer assessment, 96

CAPTR teaming, 90

CAPTR team methodology, 87

CAPTR team model, 85

CAPTR team paradigm, 86

CAPTR team recommendations, 96

Case files backup, 88

Certification frameworks, 141, 142

© Dr. Jacob G. Oakley, Michael Butler, Wayne York, Dr. Matthew Puckett, Dr. J. Louis Sewell 2022
J. G. Oakley et al., *Theoretical Cybersecurity*, https://doi.org/10.1007/978-1-4842-8300-4

U

V

W, X, Y

Z

Printed in the United States
by Baker & Taylor Publisher Services

Theoretical Cybersecurity

There is a distinct lack of theoretical innovation in the cybersecurity industry. This is not to say that innovation is lacking, as new technologies, services, and solutions (as well as buzzwords) are emerging every day. This book will be the first cybersecurity text aimed at encouraging abstract and intellectual exploration of cybersecurity from the philosophical and speculative perspective. Technological innovation is certainly necessary, as it furthers the purveying of goods and services for cybersecurity producers in addition to securing the attack surface of cybersecurity consumers where able.

The issue is that the industry, sector, and even academia are largely technologically focused. There is not enough work done to further the trade—the craft of cybersecurity. This book frames the cause of this and other issues, and what can be done about them. Potential methods and directions are outlined regarding how the industry can evolve to embrace theoretical cybersecurity innovation as it pertains to the art, as much as to the science.

To do this, a taxonomy of the cybersecurity body of work is laid out to identify how the influences of the industry's past and present constrain future innovation. Then, cost-benefit analysis and right-sizing of cybersecurity roles and responsibilities—as well as defensible experimentation concepts—are presented as the foundation for moving beyond some of those constraining factors that limit theoretical cybersecurity innovation. Lastly, examples and case studies demonstrate future-oriented topics for cybersecurity theorization such as game theory, infinite-minded methodologies, and strategic cybersecurity implementations.

What you'll learn

- The current state of the cybersecurity sector and how it constrains theoretical innovation
- How to understand attacker and defender cost benefit The detect, prevent, and accept paradigm - How to build your own cybersecurity box
- Supporting cybersecurity innovation through defensible experimentation
- How to implement strategic cybersecurity
- Infinite vs finite game play in cybersecurity

ISBN 978-1-4842-8299-1
54499

9 781484 282991

Shelve in:
Cybersecurity

User level:
Intermediate

apress®

www.apress.com